The Living Wilderness

The Living Wilderness

Earl W. Hunt

Illustrations by George Overlie

Lerner Publications Company
Minneapolis

Published simultaneously in Canada by
J. M. Dent & Sons (Canada) Ltd., Don Mills, Ontario

Library of Congress Cataloging in Publication Data

Hunt, Earl J.
  The Living Wilderness.

  SUMMARY: Describes the wildlife existing in the woodland
areas of northern United States and explores their relationship
with their environment and each other.
  1. Zoology—United States—Juvenile literature. 2. Forest
ecology—United States—Juvenile literature. [1. Forest animals.
2. Forest ecology. 3. Ecology] I. Overlie, George. II. Title.
QL155.H86   599'.09776   76-22449
ISBN 0-8225-0760-9

Manufactured in the United States of America

1 2 3 4 5 6 7 8 9 10 85 84 83 82 81 80 79 78 77

Contents

Introduction

In a remote area of north-central Minnesota, an animal trail follows the crest of a long, narrow ridge. At the end of the ridge it descends to the edge of a lake, skirts the shoreline for some distance, and then reascends to wind its way along a series of smaller ridges.

In places the trail is hardly noticeable among the dead and decaying leaves that cover the ground; in other places the ground has been marked deeply over the centuries by the four-footed creatures of the forest. Where the trail crosses a tamarack swamp, the ground is spongy and damp, cushioned by a layer of brown needles and velvety green moss. This trail is just one of a number of crisscrossing trails, many of them lesser and only occasionally used.

The central and largest body of water in the area, called Wildwood Lake, is connected to other woodland lakes by a small river. The rolling hills surrounding these lakes were once covered almost entirely with immense white pines. But after the removal of the trees by lumber companies, the hills were forested mostly with deciduous trees such as maples, oaks, and birches amid only a scattering of pines, spruces, and other evergreens. In summer, the tops of these trees form a canopy that shades the forest floor, where lichens, ferns, and mosses grow and where wild flowers bloom.

In this relatively undisturbed area, a great variety of wildlife populates the clear waters of the lakes, the lush marshes, and the green forest. In the water and along the edges of the lakes and streams are beaver and muskrat, mink and otter, raccoon and skunk, while in the forest and on its game trails can be found many of the same animals. Larger animals such as deer, bears, wolves, and foxes also roam the forest floor. Ducks and loons populate the water, while in the trees and airways are myriad songbirds and birds of prey.

The creatures in this wilderness area live out their lives with little disturbance from human beings, who only occasionally enter the area. Together, the trees, plants, and animals in the land of the woodland lakes make up an intricate web of life, a tightly knit community in which all the members are interdependent. While the animals depend upon the trees and plants for food and shelter, the plants are in turn fertilized by the soil-enriching waste matter and decomposed bodies of the animals. Some of the forest's creatures such as the rabbits, squirrels, and mice feed only on nuts and plants; others such as the owls, wolves, and foxes are meat-eaters that feed on plant-eating animals; and still others feed on both plants and animals.

The predatory animals that dwell in the land of the woodland lakes help to maintain the area's natural balance between plants and animals by keeping the plant-eating animals in check, so that their numbers remain stable. If it were not for such predators as the hawk and the eagle, the bobcat and the lynx, the populations of some plant-eating animals would soon double in size. They would rapidly strip the land of its vegetation, and widespread famine would result. The balance of nature would be upset, and the lives of all the other creatures in the forest would be endangered.

The whole community of living things in the land of the woodland lakes is greatly affected by the seasonal changes that occur there. Each of the four seasons brings changes in the area's plant life, with resultant changes in the lives of the animals. Spring is a time of reawakening and rebirth, summer a time of warmth and growth. Autumn brings blazing colors and a time for harvesting, whereas winter, with its severe cold and its scarcity of food, can be a real challenge for the young, the old, the weak.

For many of the creatures of the wild, it is a very difficult life. For all, it is difficult at times. Although there is often danger and fear, there is never hatred. There sometimes is hunger and starving, but there is no self-pity. Despite all hardships and problems, to be wild and free and alive is a supreme pleasure to the animals that make their homes in the land of the woodland lakes.

Part I

❧

Spring and Summer

SPRING, THE SEASON OF REAWAKENING AND NEW LIFE, COMES late to the forests of Minnesota. But by June, summer is in full stride and activity is everywhere. It is a time of rearing, for into the short summer must be crowded all the growing, learning, and developing that will be required of each young creature if it is to survive in a hostile world. The severeness of the coming winter will test how well each has learned through the summer. But summer is also a time for playing and frolicking and for enjoying the bounty that nature has provided.

The Great Horned Owl

FROM HIS VANTAGE POINT ON THE LIMB OF A DEAD PINE TREE, a great horned owl surveyed the surrounding woodland with piercing eyes. It was dusk, and he had just wakened from his daily sleep in a dense Norway pine thicket, one of the half dozen roosting places in his territory.

He was a majestic bird, standing two feet tall, but with a broad, massive body that gave him the appearance of being even larger than he was. When his wings were outstretched, they measured almost five feet from tip to tip—a wingspread as great as that of any other owl in the forest. The two black-feathered ear tufts on his head explained why he was called a "horned" owl. His large yellow eyes were almost half filled with black pupils in the fading light. With increased darkness, there would be almost no yellow left as the pupils expanded to gather in as much light as possible, so that this skilled hunter could see well even on moonless nights or when there was an overcast sky. A heavy, curved beak completed the owl's facial makeup. Brown feathers, lighter on his chest and legs, covered even his feet, outfitting the owl for cold weather survival. Only the four curved talons on each foot protruded from the insulating feathers.

Behind him on the forest floor, a deer mouse rustled some dry leaves. Instantly the owl's head swiveled 180 degrees around, his ear tufts held high and his muscles poised for action. The faintest rustling came again, and he cranked his head still farther to pinpoint the source. With immovable eyes fixed in their sockets, the owl could change his field of vision only by moving his head. But this was compensated for by very flexible neck vertebrae that enabled him to turn his head nearly three-fourths of the way around, so that he could look straight over his back.

For a moment, the white-footed mouse showed itself above the cover of leaves. Swiftly the hunting bird leaped from his perch, his soundless wings carrying him directly to the target. Only a short squeak of protest was uttered before the owl's sharp talons brought a quick end to the victim's life.

The owl flew back to his perch on the pine tree, and, with one gulp, the mouse was swallowed whole. Immediately the owl's attention was turned toward finding more food to satisfy his nearly insatiable appetite. When five minutes passed without a sign of anything to eat, the owl sent out a series of loud hoots that reverberated across the land. The noise froze all the small animals in the area into silent fear. Again came the loud, frightening cry of the owl. Every mouse, rabbit, and flying squirrel, every small nocturnal creature within hearing distance, dove for cover or remained hidden as the terror of the night broadcast his claim over his kingdom. It would be some time before the preyed-upon animals of the woodland would again venture out in their own quests for food.

When he had finished hooting, the great horned owl left his perch in the pine and flew away. His hooting had served as a warning to other owls that this piece of real estate belonged exclusively to him and that trespassing would not be tolerated. (Indeed, he would bring down his wrath on even his own offspring if they should now dare to trespass.) Now that the owl had driven everything into hiding, he winged his way over wooded hills to the edge of a lake.

The owl knew almost every inch of the large expanse of land and water that he claimed as his own. Although he sometimes hunted on wing, he preferred to watch from some high perch where his piercing eyes could search out anything that moved. One of these perches was a large, leafless birch tree that had been dead for nearly two years. With only the large limbs remaining, but with all the white bark intact, it still stood majestically after death. Since the tree leaned out over an expanse of shallow water from a swamp below, it served as a good perch from which to keep watch for creatures that the great horned owl might find tasty.

From this stately birch skeleton, the night hunter watched patiently for almost an hour before the surface of the shallow water was broken by a young muskrat. Soon two more appeared, and the three fed on the vegetation that grew in profusion in the muddy water. After a while, the little muskrats climbed onto dry ground and began playing, chasing each other through the weeds, pouncing on one another, and tumbling back into the water.

The owl saw every movement the muskrats made, from the moment the first one rippled the water. He was sure that at any moment he could easily pick off one of the unsuspecting creatures, but the gnawing hunger in his stomach told him to wait until he could get all three. So he waited anxiously for his prey to move away from the safety of the water, his shoulders and head leaning forward and his muscles poised for flight.

Several times, two of the long-tailed rodents moved dangerously far from the water; and, more than once, the owl nearly took flight. When one of the muskrats entered the water and swam away beneath the surface, the owl became alarmed that all three would leave. He flew swiftly to the pair that still frolicked and silently grabbed one of them up. Its squeal was cut short by the owl's plunging talons, but the alarm lasted long enough to send the other muskrat fleeing toward the water. Knowing that the first one was dead, the owl dropped it and raced after its companion. Closing talons caught one of its hind legs just as the second muskrat dove beneath the water's surface. For a brief moment there was a fierce struggle, with flying water, beating wings, angry cries, and snapping jaws. Soon all was quiet again. The little muskrat had never really had a chance.

Three more mice, a shrew, and a small bird fell prey to the great horned owl that night before he again took refuge in the Norway thicket at dawn to sleep out the day. This was a pattern that had been carried out almost every day of the owl's life. He had been hatched two and a half years earlier on the last day of February, months before most bird eggs are laid. Two years later, he had himself helped to raise a pair of young. . .

Although he was good sized for a male great horned owl, his mate had been even larger. At first she had watched quietly and with little apparent interest as he had danced, bobbed, and bounced in the snow and from tree to stump to tree, flapping his wings ridiculously and clicking his beak loudly and rapidly. Finally she had become impressed with his acrobatics and had gone nest building with him.

They had taken over an abandoned nest in a forked limb high up in a hickory tree. They had added strong twigs to it, weaving them into the nest until it was solid enough to meet their needs. Two round, cream-colored eggs had then been laid, and thereafter had been kept warm by the two parents, who had taken turns sitting on the eggs and protecting them from the elements. In spite of the below-zero temperatures and the howling winds and snow, both eggs had hatched and the young had thrived. By the time most other birds' eggs had begun hatching, the two owlets had been ready to strike out on their own.

. . . When the big male owl awoke from his sleep in the Norway thicket and stretched his wings, the daylight was gone. The first thing he did was to relieve himself of a large quantity of digested material. Next he hunched over and regurgitated a large oblong pellet, followed by another one, each of them about three inches long. These were compressed masses of bones, fur, scales, and feathers that had been rolled and packed into firm pellets in the owl's stomach. Since many of his victims—particularly the small ones— were swallowed whole, this was the owl's way of getting rid of the materials he could not digest.

Although he had eaten over half his own weight in food the previous night, the owl was already very hungry. He weighed just over four pounds with a completely empty stomach; but keeping his stomach full was what most of the predator's life was directed toward. This evening the owl had awakened later than usual, for already it was quite dark. He winged his way through the woods like a black shadow, maneuvering through the intertwining branches without ever touching one. Hardly a trace of sound marked his flight as he moved silently on wings designed not to betray his coming. The soft, downy projections on the fringes of his feathers served as near-perfect mufflers, so that air passing over the feathers made hardly a whisper of sound.

Three-quarters of a mile away, upstream from Wildwood Lake, the night hunter stopped at the edge of a smaller lake. There a tall, lifeless elm tree leaned out over the water. The tree had been dead for three years, and yet it still stood solidly, its leafless branches reaching 60 feet over the water's surface. From this lofty perch, the owl had sailed forth to snatch up many a muskrat as it floated on the water, or to grab up a mouse or a squirrel as it came to the lake for a drink. Tonight all was still. The keen-eyed bird of prey kept watch in the elm for a long time, waiting expectantly for something to move, occasionally preening his feathers with a deft stroke of his beak.

Finally, a movement a hundred yards down the shore attracted the owl's attention. A family of striped skunks, a mother and her four kits, had come to the lake to drink and to look for food. When the owl first spotted them, they were yet a few feet back from the water, digging up angleworms, grubs, and other juicy tidbits. A while later, they moved on to the water's edge for a drink. Suddenly the old skunk detected something that excited her: telltale tracks in the sandy beach and the faint smell of turtle. She began digging briskly, and soon she unearthed about two dozen turtle eggs that had been deposited and buried in the sand the day before.

The eggs, looking more like ping-pong balls than anything else, were a feast for the family of five. In the midst of the feast, however, feathered fury dropped out of the sky. A loud, growling warning note from the old one sent the four kits ambling for cover. They did not go swiftly, for they had learned that the protective spray they carried was a defensive weapon that would stop almost any enemy from pursuing them.

The owl came in fearlessly, seizing and holding one of the kits, undaunted by the foul-smelling liquid that it and its mother sprayed at him. Standing on the ground, he swallowed the young skunk in one gulp. The pungent defensive spray, called musk and capable of causing a wolf or a fox to vomit, did not seem to bother the owl at all, though his feathers would reek of it for several days. After the four surviving skunks had disappeared, their attacker feasted on the delectable turtle eggs they had left behind.

A short time later, after returning to his perch, the owl spied the bobbing figure of a slim, weasel-like animal along the shore. It was swift and agile, and its dark-brown fur looked pure black in the bright moonlight. Instantly the owl sprang from the elm tree and hurtled toward the moving figure, his legs outstretched and his murderous talons poised for the strike. But a fraction of a second before the owl reached his target, the intended victim leaped into a hollow log and disappeared. Frustrated, the owl flew off to another roost, knowing that waiting for the animal to reappear would be useless.

The owl had made many attempts at catching the cunning animal with the dark-brown fur. Many times he had come within a breath of snatching it up, but each time capture had been avoided by the animal's split-second maneuvering. The owl had good reason for wanting to catch this particular animal—a reason that went beyond the usual one of wanting to eat it. For the animal was a mink, a flesh-eating mammal that ate all the creatures the owl did. The owl and the mink were competing with each other for the same food, and the owl didn't like the competition.

The winged hunter did not fly back to his perch on the dead elm, for he knew that game was usually hard to find after the mink had passed through an area. Some distance away, the owl came to a grassy meadow where a great number of meadow mice lived. A maze of tiny paths crisscrossed one another where the mice traveled about through the grass. Catching the little rodents was not easy despite their large population, however, because most of their paths were concealed beneath the grass. And even when the mice were out in the open, they could quickly find cover in the nearby grass and shrubs. The owl began hunting them by using a low-level flight, just above the grass, so that he could dive the moment a mouse exposed itself. But this tiresome method netted the owl only three mice in two hours, and it burned up almost as much energy as the mice provided.

The following night the owl rested atop a small basswood stump, about 12 feet off the ground, as he watched a pair of young cottontails playing and feeding at the edge of a hazel thicket. With a full moon overhead, the owl was able to see every movement the rabbits made. He viewed them intently, waiting for them to wander out from under the thick bushes so that he could pounce on them. Three times he nearly left the stump, but each time the prey moved back to the safety of the thick shrubbery.

Finally one of the rabbits moved a hop farther out, and the big bird swooped silently down. As he drifted in for the kill, his shadow moved ahead of him to alert the rabbit, sending the intended victim bolting for cover. By the barest of margins, the rabbit escaped as a razor-sharp talon raked across its back. But its scream startled the other rabbit, and it darted out in front of the owl. With instant reflexes, the bird banked and swerved, and this time he did not miss. Powerful leg muscles sunk the talons in deeply, and the squealing and kicking rabbit was lifted easily off the ground. Almost instantly, the life left it.

Back on the basswood stump, the owl took the victim in his beak and leaned back, with his head held high. He swallowed three times, and the rabbit was inside him, all in one piece.

Except for the small rabbit, it was a fruitless night for the great horned owl. As the morning sunlight began sifting in, he was still very hungry. The sun was well above the trees when he finally flew toward a resting spot for sleep. While winging his way over a hazelbrush thicket on a hillside, he spotted several small wolf cubs playing beside the thick bushes. As his outstretched feet struck a victim, his knees were bent by the impact, an action that automatically forced the talons shut. Powerful wingbeats lifted the screaming whelp and carried it away as the other young wolves scrambled for their den.

This was one of the rare occasions on which the owl was unable to swallow his prey whole. After carrying it for some distance, he settled onto a broad stump where he tore the wolf cub apart and devoured it. With his stomach completely filled, the night hunter winged his way heavily and laboriously toward his favorite clump of Norway pines.

It was later in the day than when he usually went to sleep, and the sun was shining brightly as the owl flew past a grassy knoll. Beside the knoll he spotted an adult woodchuck, or groundhog, just as it spotted him. As the animal dove for a hole in the knoll, the owl saw that several young woodchucks were directly behind it. He plunged toward them, but his talons struck the soft dirt piled at the den's entrance just as the last woodchuck disappeared inside.

The near miss did not greatly disturb the owl. His cavernous stomach was full. He felt satisfied from the recent meal and was very tired from the long night of hunting. So he moved on to the seclusion of the Norway pine thicket and positioned himself on a sturdy limb among the dense needles, his shoulder beside the husky trunk. He preened his feathers by stroking them with his beak for only a moment or two before falling asleep.

The Woodchuck

THE YOUNG MALE WOODCHUCK CRIED FROM FRIGHT WHEN THE shadowy figure from above struck the dirt behind him just as he darted into the safety of his home. The cry, a sort of whimpering whistle, was repeated by the groundhog directly in front of him as they raced deeper into their underground sanctuary.

The frightened young male was not aware that he had escaped death only because the owl had just eaten. He could not have known that the extra weight in the bird's stomach had slowed down its movements, or that the full feeling in the owl's stomach had prevented it from putting the maximum effort into the attack. The woodchuck had escaped the owl's talons only because a wolf pup had given up its life earlier.

Farther into the tunnel raced the family of groundhogs. The tunnel sloped steeply down for the first few feet and then leveled off. About 12 feet in, a small room lay off to one side. The room was somewhat higher than the rest of the tunnel, a neat piece of engineering that the mother woodchuck had built into the home. Since the burrow lay in a hillside with good drainage, there was little chance of its flooding; and, if somehow flooding should occur, the higher room would still remain dry. This split-level house had been planned well.

The four youngsters stopped in the bedroom, which was carpeted with a soft layer of grass and leaves. They lay there, whimpering softly, while their mother continued on, past a second room, to another exit-entrance hole. This one did not have a pile of dirt around it to mark it. Instead, it was concealed among tall grass and weeds.

Sitting up on her haunches, the old female woodchuck cautiously peered out of this hidden observation point and saw that the owl was already winging out of sight. Assured that the danger was gone for the present, she again led her youngsters out into the world.

The quadruplets had been born in early May. Weighing less than two ounces each, hairless and blind, they had not seen the outside world for some time. Eventually, their diet of milk had been supplemented with clover, alfalfa, and other plants that their mother had brought them. Soon after that, she had led them out to search for their own plants.

The first food-gathering trips had taken the young woodchucks only a few yards from the burrow. While the youngsters had foraged and fed, their mother had watched and listened for any sign of danger. It was natural for the young ones to mimic their parent, and her watchfulness had taught them to be constantly on guard. Occasionally, even though she had detected no danger, she had suddenly run for the burrow opening. Her offspring had scurried after her, quickly learning that safety was their underground home.

It was on their fourth day out that the owl had struck in the forenoon. When the old woodchuck led her brood out later that day, they were a little more reluctant to follow her, for they had learned that danger was not just a game to be played among mother and children. The young male woodchuck who had been last into the burrow had been so shaken by the owl's sneak attack that he now hung back behind the others, prepared to be the first one underground when the next raid occurred. Already, experience had made the little woodchuck a wiser, more cautious animal.

Danger did not strike again that day, and on successive days the fearful little groundhog fed outside with the others, usually in the forenoon and again in the late afternoon. He enjoyed clover, alfalfa, dandelions, and nearly all kinds of broad-leaved weeds, though he did not find grass to his liking. He consumed these plants in huge quantities, adding length and weight to his frame every day.

A week had passed since the owl's attack, and the young woodchuck had become braver and more relaxed, when another event occurred that was to leave a lasting impression on him. His mother spotted a red fox while it was still a considerable distance away, and she immediately gave her warning whistle. They all made it safely into the burrow, but the fox did not give up as easily as the owl had. It began digging at the burrow's entrance, its front feet tearing away the loose soil, enlarging the opening so that the fox could move the entire length of its body into the hole.

The strong smell of the fox drifted down through the tunnel as the woodchuck family crouched below in fear. To the young male woodchuck who had been so frightened before, the smell of the fox was an odor that he would never forget. Eventually, the fox tired from the digging. Seeing that any further excavation was blocked by several large rocks that lay alongside the tunnel, it gave up and moved on to search for other prey.

On subsequent days the young woodchucks began moving out farther from their burrow. The good food nearby had been cropped closely, and so they found it necessary to make long excursions to find the leafy green plants they enjoyed. At first they traveled in close company, but, as more days passed, they began venturing out alone. It was on one of these trips that the young male got an opportunity to use some of his stored knowledge.

He was farther from home than he had ever been before, and was munching on some tender plantain, when his sensitive nose detected something that stopped his chewing. The odor became stronger, and a second whiff of it sent panic through him. It was the the smell of fox! The woodchuck wanted to break and run, but the burrow was much too far away for that. So he did the only other thing he knew. He lay quietly in the weeds, waiting for the danger to pass, watching every movement the fox made, knowing that he might have to flee at any moment.

The fox had gone almost a dozen yards past him, and the woodchuck was beginning to breathe a bit easier, when the fox suddenly paused and doubled back in the woodchuck's direction. The trembling woodchuck watched the fox sniffing and pawing in the grass under a bush, and then heard some whimpering sounds and a tiny squeal. Suddenly he saw an animal with a furry body, long ears, and a short, fluffy tail. Instead of running on all four legs, this animal hopped on its hind legs, which were longer than its front legs. It was smaller than the fox, and yet the animal boldly charged at the fox and kicked it. The fox was stunned by this surprise attack; but then, out of nowhere, a second fox came to its aid, grabbing the small, fluffy-tailed animal from behind and killing it. Moments later the two foxes were frightened by a noise, and they immediately ran away. The woodchuck saw them leave, but still he did not move from his hiding place. A while later, when he was sure that the danger had passed, he darted out of the weeds and raced back to the safety of his underground home.

The Cottontail

For the tiny cottontail, life had begun under a thick clump of willow bushes. Along with four brothers and sisters, he was born in a grassy nest on a warm summer afternoon. The sun was shining brightly that afternoon, but he did not see the light of day until a week later when his eyes first opened.

Several days before he arrived, his mother had dug out a shallow hole, about seven inches across, in the soft ground under the willow bushes. She then lined it with grass and with soft fur that she had pulled from her own breast, making a comfortable nest for her young. When the five kits were born, she licked each one clean and then carried them one at a time to the waiting nest, only three feet away, where they received their first meal of milk.

The little cottontail and his brothers and sisters had not been very attractive at first. Born hairless and pink skinned, they were less than two inches long and weighed only a quarter of an ounce. But despite their homely appearance, they were the most important thing in the world to their mother. This was her second brood of the season, and she would likely have one more before the summer ended; but for now, these five kits were all that mattered to her. Each time she left them during the first few days, she covered the nest with grass in order to hide her babies and to keep them warm. The newborn rabbits were always anxious for their meal of milk, and they uttered small cries of anticipation

when they heard her return.

After their eyes had opened, the old doe had taken them out of the nest once a day for a short outing so that they could begin nibbling on green food and become accustomed to the larger environment. The kits were just 12 days old when the slaughter occurred. Their mother had left them in the nest for a while, and a red fox passed by the bush in which the nest was concealed. A faint whiff of rabbit scent touched its nose, and automatically the fox doubled back toward the bush. Sniffing and pawing in the grass, it uncovered the nest in which the five kits huddled. Quickly one was grabbed up. It let out a tiny squeal before the fox's sharp canine teeth closed, and then it went limp.

As the fox reached into the nest for a second kit, it saw a brown blur out of the corner of its eye. The mother rabbit, returning home, had heard the squeal, and she now defied all the odds by charging at the intruder. She whirled around in midair and kicked the fox with her powerful hind feet, thumping it soundly on the side of the neck.

The fox was stunned. Rabbits had always run from him. He had never known one to charge him, or even to stand and fight. But, then, he had never before encountered a mother rabbit while he was trying to steal her young. Before he could recover, he received another blow—this time directly in the face, one claw drawing blood just above the eye and coming dangerously close to blinding that eye. The rabbit might have won out against the nearly impossible odds—might actually have driven the fox away and moved her babies to safety—had she not been outnumbered. For *two foxes* had been hunting together, traveling a short distance apart, and the second one now joined the fight, grabbing the gallant rabbit from behind.

Having killed the mother rabbit, the foxes turned their attention to the young kits in the nest. In the scuffle, the nest had been torn up and the young had been scattered. Two of them were quickly found and consumed, but the other two had been thrown some distance away and now lay huddled in the grass, motionless. The foxes continued searching for more kits and likely would have found the two that crouched in fear had not a moose come trotting along, crashing through the brush. The noise sent the foxes fleeing ahead of the moose without even waiting to see what kind of animal it was.

For hours the two surviving kits, one male and one female, remained hidden in the tall grass. They had already gone without eating for a long time when the fox first appeared, and now the great hunger in them finally forced them to move. There would be no more milk for the kits, and they were not yet used to eating only vegetation. Completely inexperienced at surviving in a hostile world, and with no mother to teach them how to avoid some of the countless enemies and dangers they would face, the young cottontails would be lucky if they lived another day or two.

They moved slowly and cautiously, never venturing more than a few steps from each other. Before long they came to a patch of vegetation that would be digestible even to their underdeveloped stomachs. It was a patch of white clover— tender green stems with small white blossoms that tasted as sweet as they smelled. As the two rabbits continued on their way, they sampled other green leafy plants, including some wild sweet peas that were just beginning to open their blossoms.

As night fell on the land of the woodland lakes, the young cottontails bedded down in a thick growth of ferns that concealed them entirely. They slept there again the following night, adopting the fern patch as their home. The thick, arching ferns bent all the way to the ground, so that the two rabbits could not be seen from above or even from ground level. Another advantage of the fern patch was that it had many exits, so that the cottontails could not be cornered by an animal sealing off the escape route. The only danger was that an enemy might stumble into the fern patch—a possibility the two rabbits were constantly on the alert for.

The first time an approaching animal alarmed them was when a mallard led her newly hatched ducklings past the fern patch on her way to the lake. The two cottontails first heard and then saw the strange-looking birds moving slowly along, heading straight toward them. The trembling rabbits huddled in fear as the mallards approached. But as they studied the shapes and movements of the flat-billed birds, the rabbits sensed that the mallards were no threat to them, and they relaxed. When the mother and her nine little ones waddled on past the fern patch, the two cottontails looked on more with curiosity than with anxiety. Over the centuries, cottontails had learned that ducks do not eat rabbits, and this information had somehow been stored in their brains, passed on to them from their parents, who had inherited the instinct and observed the fact.

Many days later, when the rabbits were feeding along the shore of the lake, they again saw the family of mallards, though now there were only three young following the mother instead of nine. The rabbits could not count, but it was obvious to them that the family was smaller now than before. Just as in their own family, the mallards' numbers had been greatly reduced by animals who must eat meat in order to stay alive.

The young cottontails had been robbed of parental security too early in life, and, with everything else gone, they had taken comfort in each other. A close bond had formed between brother and sister, and the one never ventured far without the other. Each day, however, their foraging trips took them farther and farther from home. One night they discovered a low, boggy meadow beyond the lake where broad-leaved swamp grass grew in profusion and where trails meandered and crisscrossed among the grass. Clumps of pussy willow and speckled alder bushes grew here and there, making a dense cover to hide under, and there were many kinds of leafy green plants to feast upon. Before long the rabbits were full from eating and weary from playing and running. When they entered the fern patch just before daylight, they carried a pleasant feeling with them.

The following night found the two cottontails at the edge of a dense hazelbrush thicket. They would move out from under the bushes to feed awhile, and then would hop back to safety. A full moon was shining over the lake. From the protection of the hazelbrush, the young male rabbit stared at the orange moon and its sparkling reflection in the ripples of the lake. Then he moved out and began nibbling on a wild daisy. Moments later, the rabbit glanced up to see a dark shadow cover the moon, and he bolted toward the bushes—

but not quite in time. The talons of a great horned owl raked across his back, ripping a long gash. The wounded cottontail squealed in terror and pain as he rushed into cover. His scream in turn terrified the young female rabbit, and she bolted out into the open, exposing herself to the owl. A split second after the owl had lost its hold on the one rabbit, another was unexpectedly in its flight path! The bird's instantaneous reflexes brought the talons of both feet into an unbreakable hold on the violently kicking victim. From his hiding place in the bushes, the little male cottontail watched as his sister was swept away by the fearsome night hunter.

Thus he became the sole survivor of a family of cottontails that had once numbered six, a story that is repeated countless times every year—and necessarily so. An adult female cottontail usually raises three litters a year, with an average of six kits per litter, so that if all survived, a pair of rabbits would become 20 after one year. The next year, if each pair became 20 more and if all survived, the number would reach 200; and in the third year, 2,000. After six years, if all survived and continued to produce at the same rate, the original pair of cottontails and their offspring would number in the millions. Before long, the world would be overrun with rabbits.

But nature has planned that the world shall not be overrun with rabbits, and so it is that a host of predatory animals prey on them. The tireless weasels and mink seek them out. The bobcats and lynx hide in ambush and pounce on them. The hawks and eagles hurtle out of the sky by day, and the silent and merciless owls by night. The foxes and wolves run them down, and other flesh-eating animals catch them by one means or another. To stay alive, then, each rabbit must remain constantly alert. Survival of the species depends mainly on speed, agility, and fertility.

The male rabbit did not fully understand death, but he sensed that he would never again see his sister and constant companion. Feeling very much alone, he stayed close to the security of the ferns for several days. It was summertime— the time of abundance—and green plants grew everywhere. So the rabbit had no problem satisfying his enormous appetite, and the rapidly growing youngster consumed almost half his weight in plants every day.

Strawberries had ceased to bear, but raspberries were now ripening, and the rabbit varied his diet of grass and leaves by munching some of the red fruit. In doing so, the cottontail was unknowingly providing a service to nature, for many of the tiny berry seeds passed through his system undigested. These seeds were returned to the soil to sprout new berry plants, and along with each seed was deposited some nutritious fertilizer to help it grow. This method of sowing spread the seeds throughout the forest.

Every day the cottontail came across hundreds of mice. Their large numbers never disturbed him, though, for he merely ignored them. But ignoring them became impossible when a female deer mouse decided to build her nest in the cottontail's fern patch. . .

IT HAPPENED ONE MORNING AFTER A BRISK SHOWER. THE sun had come out, and a supreme freshness was in the air. The small white-footed mouse had been hunting for a suitable place to build her nest, and, when she came to the fern patch and found a small stump in it, she immediately took possession. The stump was short, about a foot high and almost as wide. The fact that the arching ferns hid it almost entirely from the air was the major factor in the mouse's decision to stay.

Three days later the top of the stump held a finished nest.

The deer mouse had constructed it of grass, strips of bark, and plant fibers, carefully weaving them into a sturdy structure that included even a waterproof roof. A small opening near the bottom allowed the mouse to enter the nest. The final touch was to line it with soft thistle and dandelion down, so that her young would be comfortable when they came into the world.

The mouse had done all this work while her body was still heavy with young. The day after completing the nest, she gave birth to six baby mice. Within the cottontail's fern patch there now lived a family of animals that were much more prolific than the rabbit was. Their rate of maturity and reproduction was such that a mouse born in April could have 200 great-grandchildren by October. No wonder they were the most numerous animals in the woods!

Although the mother deer mouse was a strikingly beautiful animal whose white-and-brown coloring and large ears and eyes made her look like a miniature deer, her six infants were not at all pretty. They were pink, hairless, and blind, with a blue membrane that stretched over their bulging eyeballs. Yet they were the pride and joy of their mother. Tenderly and affectionately, she cleaned and washed them, often picking one up in her front paws or rolling it over, and then allowing it to nurse.

If the cottontail resented sharing his home with these strange-looking creatures, he did not show it. Knowing that the mother and her young meant him no harm, he left them alone and kept to himself. Over the next two weeks, the mother deer mouse was constantly on the move, leaving the nest several times a day to look for berries, nuts, seeds, and small insects. Each time she returned to the nest, she was greeted by the high-pitched squeaks of her young, who were eager for her milk and the warm softness of her body.

At two weeks of age, the tiny deer mice were old enough to

be weaned, and it was their mother's intention to nurse them for the last time when she returned home from one of her short food-gathering trips. But that intention was shattered the moment she entered the ferns. She froze, only a few feet from the stump, as she saw her nest being ravaged by a mink. It had torn the nest open, grabbing up all the young mice before they could escape. Their mother now watched, horrified, as the mink devoured them.

She remained where she was, crouched against some fern stems, for about an hour. Finally she moved to the nest, inspecting it and searching for survivors. But the destruction was complete. Leaving the fern patch behind, the female deer mouse at once set out to look for another mate. She would find one that day, and, three weeks later, she would give birth to another batch of young. She would not return to the fern patch, however, for cleanliness was of prime importance to her, and she would not even consider rearing a second litter in the same nest.

The cottontail was once again the sole inhabitant of the fern patch. He had been asleep when the mink had entered his home and killed the mice. He had awoken moments after the mink had left the fern patch, carrying the last one in its mouth. The presence of the mouse nest had probably saved the rabbit's life, for had the mink not been attracted to the nest, it might have continued on to where the rabbit lay sleeping.

SINCE LOSING HIS SISTER TO THE GREAT HORNED OWL, THE young cottontail had narrowly escaped death several more times, and each time he had become a little wiser. In open areas, he had learned not to travel far in a straight line without zigzagging left and right or leaping to one side and darting off in another direction. These were elusive tactics

that could foil the plans of a diving bird of prey. Whenever the cottontail spotted a hawk or an owl in the sky, he would immediately stop and hide under any kind of concealment he could find—a bush or a windfall or a clump of dead grass into which his gray-brown fur would blend perfectly.

When he found himself close to danger, the rabbit would put his limitless patience to work, lying close to the ground, his ears pinned back, with nothing moving except his twitching nose. If the danger came too close, even the nose would stop moving. His eyes, located on the sides of his head rather than directly in front, gave him great peripheral vision. Without moving his head, he could see both sides plainly; and, with his ears held back, he could see all but a small section directly behind him. His sharp eyes could take in all of the sky as well, and more than once this saved him from being dinner for some hungry hawk.

But if he should be discovered in spite of his protective coloration and his stillness, his powerful hind legs would instantly burst into a high-speed hop. As he bolted away from his pursuer, the furry white underside of his tail would look like a bouncing ball of cotton. It seemed that nature had played a cruel trick in giving him the flashing white tail, but it was often a blessing in disguise. For the pursuer would almost always focus on the bouncing patch of white. When the cottontail sat down and the white disappeared, the pursuer's eyes would look beyond him in search of his tail. It took all these tricks and more to keep the cottontail alive.

Yet the rabbit's worst problem for this time of year was not the fear of predators but the suffering and misery caused by the countless parasites that preyed on him. Mosquitoes, flies, and other insect pests were constantly after his blood. His thick fur helped to protect his body from these thieves, but it provided a 24-hour home for fleas, lice, and other bloodsucking pests. In addition to these parasites, there were the terrible botflies, the mites, the wood ticks, the liver flukes, the intestinal worms, and many others, most of which the rabbit had little or no defense against.

But the young cottontail accepted it all, remaining reasonably happy and at peace with himself, enjoying the flavors of the greenery around him, eating almost continuously from the banquet that nature provided. As the days and weeks passed, the rabbit grew larger, stronger, and wiser. The terrible gash he had received on his back from the great horned owl gradually healed, leaving only a long white scar to show where the owl's talons had raked across him.

With the arrival of late summer, the leaves of some trees were already beginning to turn from green to yellowish green to yellow. The wild rice plants that grew in the shallow waters of the lakes and ponds, swamps and marshes, were now several feet above the water. Back in the spring, when the plants were young, the rice beds had looked like bright-green lakes; but now, as the rice plants began to ripen and turn gold, they looked more like wheat fields. These aquatic plants were as delicious as the choicest grass, and birds of many species moved into the rice beds to feed on the swollen kernels.

As he hopped along the shore of a woodland lake, the cottontail saw great numbers of red-winged blackbirds feeding on the rice. Spreading their wings to show their brilliant red-and-yellow wingbars, they flitted from plant to plant, teetering precariously on the swaying stalks while they ate the seeds and consumed the tiny white worms that were also feeding on the rice. Their constant chattering disturbed the rabbit, and yet he knew that the blackbirds were no threat to him.

Following the shoreline, the cottontail came to the narrow, swampy end of the lake where the water was shallow and where wild rice grew in abundance. Mallards and teals, coots and wood ducks, were floating on the water, feeding on the nourishing rice. A little farther out, in deeper water, bluebills and canvasbacks were diving for the fallen kernels that lay on the lake bottom. Fortunately, enough of the fertile seeds would remain hidden in the mud so that this life-sustaining plant could grow and produce for another year, furnishing the creatures of the woodland lakes with another rich harvest of rice.

A scattering of rice plants grew along the lake's boggy border, near the place where a small river entered the lake. The rabbit fed on the stalks and kernels that were within his reach, finding them delicious; but he did not go into the lake after more. Beside the rabbit, at the edge of the water, was a cone-shaped pile of weeds, grass, and mud. Just as he was about to return to his fern patch, the cottontail noticed something lying on the surface of the lake a few feet off shore, not far from him. It was a muskrat, floating motionless on the water, looking straight back at him. For minutes they stared at each other, neither one of them posing a threat to the other and neither one displaying any fear.

Along the water's edge, some 200 feet away, a dark-brown animal with a slender body and a long, bushy tail quietly moved along, sniffing and poking at every object and cavity that it passed. As the animal approached, the rabbit's peripheral vision detected its movement, and the rabbit turned his head in that direction. Immediately the muskrat's eyes followed. The rabbit and the muskrat both panicked, for the dark-brown animal was an adult mink—one of the predators they feared most. Without hesitation, the muskrat dove and swam while the rabbit bounded off at high speed in a frantic, erratic run. The cottontail would make it home safely, surviving this latest brush with death, for the mink had not seen him.

The Muskrat

As THE MUSKRAT SWAM AWAY, SHE STAYED WELL BENEATH the surface of the water, heading straight out from shore, weaving her way through the rice stalks. She had wisely moved away from the shoreline before the mink had begun patrolling the area, for she was a crafty old female who had learned enough tricks to stay alive for several years.

She swam with powerful strokes from her back legs, propelled by large hind feet that were partially webbed, steered by a long, flattened tail that she used as a rudder. She kept one front foot tucked up under her chin as she swam. She did not have to bother with the other one, for her right front foot was gone. When only a year and a half old, she had been caught in a trap. She had struggled for hours to free herself, biting at the steel jaws that held her foot and frantically pulling at the chain with all her strength, but the trap would not release its grip.

As exhaustion had set in, her foot and leg had become

numb. The temperature was well below freezing, and the cold steel of the trap drained the warmth from her foot. In final desperation, with numbness to help mask the pain, she had begun chewing the foot off. Her earlier wrenching and twisting had severed the bone, and her sharp incisors now tore away the remaining flesh and hide, leaving the merciless trap holding only her lifeless foot.

Dazed and exhausted, and in a state of shock, she had swum slowly to her den, where she lay for days while the leg healed. The den was a burrow that she had dug in the bank of a river, with a small room above the water level where she lived and slept. It served as a warm, cozy retreat for her while her body repaired the damage. The den had two narrow tunnels or exits that opened under water, so that she could enter the river even when it was covered with ice. The second exit gave her an escape route that she could use if a mink or some other predator should enter the first tunnel to make a meal out of her. With one foot missing, and in her weakened condition, she was extremely vulnerable to attack. Of all her enemies, the mink was the one that posed the greatest danger to her, for it was slender enough to squeeze through the same tunnels that the muskrat used. What is more, the mink was so fast and powerful that not even a *healthy* muskrat could hope to outrace or outfight it.

With nothing to eat inside the den, the weak and starving muskrat was finally forced to go out on the fifth day in search of food. She slowly made her way through one of the narrow tunnels that led from her den out into the open river. Several short dives netted her some underwater weeds and a clam. The weeds she ate while sitting on the ice at the edge of the open water, but the clam she carried back to the den, holding it tightly against her chest with her one front foot while she swam. Although she was a plant-eating animal who lived mostly on waterweeds, the muskrat occasionally varied her diet with a snail, a crayfish, or a clam.

Gradually the injury healed, and the muskrat adapted to a three-legged life. Her missing limb did not prevent her from finding a mate in mid-April. The two muskrats mated, and, after a brief fling in shallow water, the male abandoned her. Soon after that, the pregnant muskrat left her den in the riverbank and built a new home in the marshy end of a nearby lake.

A month after mating, she gave birth to four young muskrats—all of them blind, hairless, pink, and so tiny that they weighed less than an ounce each. Their mother devotedly cared for and nursed them. She was so caught up in her maternal duties that the muskrat never gave a thought to her missing foot, though a trace of arthritis had begun to set into the knee joint above the stump, causing some stiffness there.

After two weeks, the little muskrats opened their eyes; and before two more weeks had passed, their mother weaned them, teaching them to eat aquatic plants, berries, twigs, snails, and even small frogs. When her children were five weeks old and strong enough to strike out on their own, the muskrat drove them away. She had mated again, and she needed time to prepare for the new litter that was growing within her.

There were seven young in this litter. Eventually they, too, were gone, and the muskrat prepared for the winter by building a house of weeds and mud in the marshy part of the lakeshore. It was a cone-shaped structure about two and a half feet high, made of cattails, grass, and weeds, plastered together with mud. The two entrances were both under water so that the cold wind could not enter and so that the muskrat could always find food under the ice.

With the onset of cold weather, the arthritis in her knee became worse, working its way up into her shoulder. By midwinter there was stiffness in both shoulders, with pain accompanying every movement. Swimming for food became a chore that the muskrat did only when she was forced to.

When the spring breakup finally came, the muskrat was in very poor condition. Thin and weak from insufficient food, and with the arthritis spreading from her shoulders down into her back, she showed no interest in mating. But as the warm weather eased her stiffness, and as readily available food added weight to her frail body, she again began planning for a family. This time she did not stay in the lake where most of the other muskrats were. Instead, she moved to a swamp several hundred yards from the lake. She built a grass nest there, just three feet back from the water's edge, and in it she gave birth to a litter of three.

The food situation that summer was the best she had ever known. Pond lilies and wild celery grew in the water, and many other delicious plants covered the higher ground. She ate, nursed her young, and sunned herself on the logs that were floating in the water. The warm sun and easy living, coupled with the contentment of a happy family, brought health back into the muskrat's body. The pain and stiffness that she had endured through the winter and spring improved to the point where her arthritis was only a minor nuisance to her.

Before long the three young muskrats emerged from their cozy nest, all wide eyed and wondering at the world they saw. On a small jack pine island in the middle of the swamp, pink moccasin flowers and purple-fringed orchids bloomed. Marsh marigolds offered their green leaves above the water, and frogs and tadpoles were everywhere. The young muskrats soon learned to enjoy the swamp. They romped and played over the logs and in the water, sometimes chasing one another and sometimes chasing the frogs and tadpoles. They also played with their mother. The old female enjoyed being mauled by her young ones, but she usually remained aloof and just watched them as they frolicked.

One evening she was lazily observing her children from a log in the center of the swamp as they cavorted in the moonlight along the water's edge. Suddenly a great horned owl swooped down and swept away two of the young muskrats as their mother watched helplessly. Her peaceful life was shattered in that one fateful moment. Hours later, a mink rushed in and claimed the muskrat's last remaining offspring, leaving her childless. Cruel as it seemed, this was nature's way of keeping the muskrats under control so that their numbers did not grow too large.

During the days that followed, the three-legged female remained in the same area. She did not respond to the male muskrats who came to court her. Her three young had arrived somewhat late in the summer, and now that they were gone, she had neither the strength nor the will to raise another litter. She still sunned herself on the logs, but the sun's warmth no longer kept the stiffness from her body. Movements again became a chore for her, and she lost all interest in the swamp. She made her way back to the lake, and, after half-heartedly exploring her way around most of it, she settled into the end where a narrow river entered and where wild rice grew.

The next day she reluctantly began the arduous task of constructing a new house for the winter. She selected a spot where bog and open water met, and on that site she piled weeds, cattails, rushes, and grass. She used mud as the "mortar" to bind it all together. The muskrat worked industriously for several days, and eventually the cone-shaped mound of weeds and mud reached a height of more than two feet. Much work remained to be done: two rooms would have to be hollowed out, and two underwater entrances would have to be dug. But the muskrat was tired, and she would

leave this work for another day.

She was floating in the water, a few feet off shore, observing the results of her efforts, when a cottontail hopped alongside the mound of weeds and stopped. She watched the rabbit nibble on a few of the rice stalks that grew within its reach. Then the rabbit spotted her, and they watched each other intently, neither one of them moving. When the cottontail quickly turned its head to one side, she followed its gaze and immediately saw the object that had drawn the rabbit's attention: a bobbing, dark-brown animal. A mink!

As the cottontail turned and ran, the muskrat dove and swam beneath the surface of the water. A hundred feet out from shore, she surfaced and lay floating on the water, buoyed up by the air trapped in her fur, as motionless as a log. Her eyes followed the mink along the shore and then turned upward, scanning the sky to prevent a sneak attack from above.

The object of her attention finally moved down the shoreline and out of the sight. A little later, feeling sure that the mink had gone, the muskrat made her way back to the shore. As she swam over the glasslike surface of the lake toward the site of her new house, she thought of all the work that remained to be done if the house was to be ready in time for winter.

The Mink

THE MINK HAD NOT SEEN THE COTTONTAIL OR THE MUSKRAT. But, as he passed the spot where they had been, his sensitive nose told him of their recent presence. Their scents were familiar to him, for rabbits and muskrats were both a regular part of his diet. This was especially true of the latter: during the winter, when other kinds of prey were less available, muskrats made up more than half of the mink's diet of red meat.

The voracious, flesh-eating mink had even begun his life on a muskrat note. Along with four other kits, he had been born in a muskrat den a year and half ago, in early spring. His mother had killed the muskrats who had inhabited the den, converting their underground home into a nursery for her children. At birth, the young minks were so small that all five of them together weighed only an ounce or so. They were covered with a soft, white fuzz that soon turned to a shiny black and that gradually became a dark chocolate brown as the kits matured.

For the newborn male, who was slightly larger than his four sisters, life began in total darkness. Even if there had been some light in the underground home, he would not have detected it, for his eyes were closed and unseeing. The young mink would remain sightless for several weeks; yet he was already using his other four senses. He could feel the soft, warm bodies that were intertwined with his own tiny form, and he could smell the musklike odor of the damp, root-lined earth that encircled him. His ears detected the small chorus of whimpers uttered by his four litter-mates, and his tongue knew the taste of the warm, stomach-filling milk that he eagerly took from his mother.

At first the infant male mink slept off and on, 24 hours a day, lying just two feet beneath the blue hepaticas and yellow bellworts that blossomed on the riverbank above him. Each time he woke, it was with an empty stomach. The hungry young mammal instinctively kneaded and nuzzled the furry warmth of his mother, sucking a few drops of her nourishing milk before returning to sleep.

The male mink grew rapidly in size and strength, and before long he opened his eyes. He was perfectly content with exploring the long, dark tunnels of his underground home until one day he found his way up to the outside world. Frightened by the dazzling brightness and the deafening loudness of this unfamiliar world, the mink retreated inward. But curiosity overcame his fear, and soon he was again staring out of the burrow's exit with wonder-filled eyes. Yet he dared not leave the den.

When the old female mink began bringing meat into the den, her kits sampled it reluctantly, inspecting it for a long time before daring to take their first bites. But in a short while they learned to savor the new food, growling and hissing at one another to protect their share. When the young minks were five weeks old, their mother withdrew her milk from them, so that their diet consisted solely of meat.

The mother continued to bring meat into the den for some time. Because she never carried out the bones, feathers, and other inedible parts that were left after every meal, the den soon became a littered, foul-smelling mess. (This, in sharp contrast to the clean, tidy household that had been kept by the muskrats, the original occupants of the den.) While the young minks were still living inside the den, not yet old

47

enough to explore the world above, their father also brought them food. But after the kits were old enough and strong enough to make their way outside the den, their father abandoned them, never to return.

The young male mink was the first of the litter to swim. Swimming came so easily to him that it was almost as if he had been born knowing how. Before many more days passed, he and the others were propelling themselves through the water with ease. They were as at home in the water as they were on land. Their partially webbed hind feet drove them at great speed, and their maneuverability was something to see as they dove and twisted like corkscrews under the water.

The frisky male frolicked and fought with his sisters, tumbling on the bank and splashing in the water. As the days passed, he spent more time fighting than playing, already showing signs of the unfriendliness and hostility that would be his disposition as an adult. When fully grown, he would be hostile even to his own kind except during the mating season.

In time the mink learned to catch his own food, beginning with insects and then moving on to larger prey such as frogs, tadpoles, and crayfish. Later he added small fish and rodents (especially mice) to his menu, along with small birds that he could catch on the ground. As he became more skilled at hunting and fishing, his mother fed him less and less. The young mink was half grown now, and he weighed almost two pounds. His body was long and slender, with short, stubby legs and a long, bushy tail. His tapered neck led to a head with small, rounded ears and beady black eyes. Dark-brown fur covered all his body except for a patch of white on his chin and some small white spots on his throat and chest. The fur was warm, rich, and silky. It would become so beautiful and luxurious that its desirability would cause human beings to be the mink's number-one enemy.

With the arrival of fall, the mink left home permanently, severing all ties with his family. He traveled over a large area that encompassed several miles of ground in all directions from his birthplace. Instead of seeking a permanent home, the mink slept in hollow logs and in other animals' dens and burrows, often driving out the rightful owners. He seldom stayed in any of these temporary havens for more than a day, leaving them at night when he moved on in search of prey. Sometimes he traveled several miles in one night. He usually hunted along the rivers, lakes, and streams, where food was plentiful; and when ventured outside his own hunting territory, he rarely stayed away for more than a few days at a time.

By the time his first winter arrived, the mink had developed into a superb, highly adaptable machine. He possessed boundless energy, and he was such a strong swimmer that he could catch virtually any fish he desired. In trees he was swift and nimble, and on ground he possessed surprising speed and agility. His legs were short, but his body was so supple that he could double up the full length of it with each leap and then straighten it out into long bounds. When cornered by enemies much larger than himself, he could be a fierce and savage fighter; and when near water, he could dive without a splash and then dart away like a fish.

In the expanse of lakes and woodland in which the mink lived and hunted, a large bird of prey also made its home. It was a great horned owl. A contest developed between them because many of the animals that made up the mink's diet were also on the owl's menu. The two predators soon came to regard each other as worthy rivals. Over the months, the owl made many sneak attacks from above in an effort to eliminate the competition. But always, the mink was too alert and too quick to be taken. As winter passed, and as spring faded into summer, their paths crossed almost daily. One moonlit night, the owl picked off two of a family of three young muskrats as they romped about in a swamp. Shortly after the owl left the scene, the mink rushed in and claimed the remaining muskrat for himself.

Late summer—the season of ripening rice and quacking ducks—came. The mink continued to hunt ceaselessly along the shores of the lakes and rivers. One day, as he was patrolling the boggy end of a lake, he approached a cone-shaped mound of weeds and mud at the water's edge. Beside the mound, a cottontail stared at a floating muskrat; but, as the mink approached, they both left in haste. Although the mink saw neither of the animals, he immediately picked up their scents when he passed the spot where they had been. He did not tarry long, though, for his empty stomach was crying for food.

A mile farther on, beside the shore of another lake, the mink spotted a pair of young wolves moving through some bushes and coming straight toward him. He slipped silently into the water and disappeared before the wolves were even aware of him. The mink emerged some distance down the shore and continued searching for food. Somewhere up ahead of him, there would be fresh meat to satisfy the demanding appetite that drove him on.

The Wolves

THE TWO YOUNG WOLVES WERE PART OF A LITTER OF FIVE that had been born earlier that year in a den concealed by a hazelbrush thicket. Dug into the south slope of a hillside, the den overlooked a deep ravine. The site had been selected largely because it served as an excellent observation point, the view encompassing most of the ravine and the adjacent hillside.

Their mother had not left the wolf pups for a moment

during the first three days of their lives, during which time the pups slept around the clock, waking occasionally to suckle and to nuzzle closer for warmth. Later, when the dark-gray female left her young alone in the den from time to time, it was only for brief periods because she had no need to hunt. Buried near the den were caches of meat that her mate had brought for her and the pups. It was a simple matter for the female wolf to find the meat and to dig it up.

At first, the five pups were almost totally helpless. Their eyes were tightly sealed, and their legs were incapable of carrying them. When the pups were about a week old, their eyes opened, but even then they did not see well. Their eyes were still whitish and unfocusing, and they saw the world as if looking through frosted glasses.

Soon after their eyes cleared, the pups began exploring the area around the den. They played and tussled with one another in the leaves and grass, developing the powerful muscles and the sharp coordination that would be essential to their survival. The pups were allowed outside the den only when their mother was there to guard them; but one day they decided to go outdoors and play while the old gray wolf was gone on a hunting trip. The frisky young wolves rolled and tumbled to the edge of the hazelbrush thicket that concealed their den, exposing themselves to danger. Without warning, a great horned owl swooped down and sunk its talons into one of the unsuspecting pups, carrying it away as the victim screamed in agony. Squealing and whimpering, the other four pups tumbled over one another in their frantic race for the den, where they huddled together until their mother's return.

The nightmarish incident was soon forgotten, but the lessons that it taught were stored away and remembered by each of the four surviving pups. The young wolves had learned that the world outside their den was a hostile world; a world inhabited by murderous enemies, both seen and unseen; a world in which only the strongest and most cautious of creatures could survive. Along with this lesson in survival, the pups had learned a lesson in obedience. For in the future, whenever their mother left them alone while she hunted for food, the young wolves waited patiently inside the den, not daring to leave it until their mother returned.

One warm afternoon in late spring, the large gray wolf made her way back to the den, slowly approaching the hazel-brush thicket that concealed it. Twenty feet short of the den, she uttered a low howl. Upon hearing the familiar call, four balls of brown fur shot out of the den and charged directly at the dark-gray wolf. The lead pup helped itself to the freshly killed hare held loosely in his mother's mouth. Dragging the hare a few feet away, the pup growled and snarled to defend the prize as a second pup tried to take it away from him. The other two youngsters fed on some mice that their mother regurgitated from her throat. Eventually, the pup who had been trying to steal the hare from his brother gave up the struggle and returned to his mother to receive the only other food she could offer—her milk.

Their hunger pacified, the four brown pups sprawled out on the ground and basked in the sun while their mother kept a watchful eye on them. The young wolves napped for a long time, occasionally scratching a flea or moving back into the sunshine as the shadows of clouds passed over them. Then the restless youngsters got up and started to scuffle with one another, an activity they never seemed to tire of.

Even at this age, each of the four young pups had a distinct personality, and the differences in their character-istics were apparent. Mischief was constantly pestering and teasing the other pups. He enjoyed pouncing on anyone he caught sleeping or looking the other way. Greedy had an enormous appetite, and he would often steal the other pups' food in order to satisfy his own hunger. He also spent more time feeding on his mother's milk than the others did. Howler was the musician of the group. He took great pride in his howling, doing much more of it than anyone else in the family. And last there was Jolly, the only female in the litter. Somehow, she managed to put up with Mischief's pestering, Greedy's thievery, and Howler's noisiness without ever losing her pleasant, easygoing disposition.

From across the ravine, on a hillside adjacent to the one on which the four pups played, a huge male wolf watched the proceedings. He posed no threat to the happy family, however, for the pups were his children and their mother was his mate. A giant among wolves, he weighed about 120 pounds. He had weighed several pounds more a few weeks earlier, before he had begun the rigorous job of providing food for the newborn pups. His thick fur was almost pure white, in sharp contrast to the dark-gray coat of his mate.

Although he was 11 years old, the huge white wolf was still a masterful hunter. He was also a devoted husband and father, and would very likely remain with his mate for life.

Old White was one of the survivors in a hostile, fiercely competitive world; yet his 11 years in the wild had taken a heavy toll on him. The once-magnificent wolf was now marked and scarred from head to tail by the teeth, claws, horns, and hoofs of all the desperate victims and savage enemies he had encountered since his youth. Because of his size, speed, and strength, Old White had always been the dominant male in any pack. This meant that he had always taken the initiative in attacking and killing any animal the pack was hunting—even when it meant pitting his 120 pounds against a moose that weighed more than half a ton. After 11 years of hunting and fighting, Old White was beginning to slow down a bit; but, with any luck, he would live another 5 or 6 years.

With two adults and four fast-growing pups to feed, the wolf family's need for food was great. Fortunately, it was summer, the time of year when the forest's population was at its peak, with a new litter of young for every pair of animals of every species. Masterful hunters that they were, the wolves were able to pick off all the animals they needed. In doing this, the wolves fit into nature's broad pattern of keeping the myriad animal populations in check, so that there would be enough food for them during the winter when the food supply would be greatly reduced.

As fading daylight ushered in the first moments of twilight, a mournful howl drifted across the ravine that separated the male wolf from his family. The female wolf pointed her nose upward and howled an answer to her mate, whereupon all four of her pups gave their comical imitations of the call. (As usual, Howler's efforts at "singing" far outlasted those of the other pups.) Eager to join her mate on the other side of the ravine, the dark-gray wolf herded her youngsters into the den. Leaving the den was not easy, though, for the pups were intent on following her, and she had to nip them repeatedly to make them stay behind. Finally they reentered the den, and she was on her way.

The gray wolf scrambled down the hill and loped across the ravine, splashing through the shallow stream that ran along its bottom and slipping through the fringe of willows and speckled alders on the stream's edge. Then she trotted up the hill on the other side of the ravine, to where her mate was waiting. When she saw him wagging his tail, she dropped her head and danced up to him sideways. Then she rolled on the ground and raised her front feet in the usual greeting of wolf partners.

With each week and even with each new day, the pups became more adventurous. At six weeks of age, they were roaming the entire hillside, chasing one another, jumping, wrestling, and biting with their baby teeth. Their eyes were focusing better now, and they spent busy days attacking small sticks, shaking and growling at bones, and chasing after windblown leaves. These activities strengthened their muscles and helped to develop their hunting skills, which would have to be sharply honed if the wolves were to compete successfully against other meat-eating animals of the wild. Their attacks on leaves and sticks soon led to pouncing on grasshoppers and crickets—their first conquests. Later, as the hunter within each of them awakened, the young wolves killed their first real animals. For Mischief, it was a mouse; for Greedy, a small shrew; for Howler and Jolly, a frog.

To these wolf pups enjoying their first summer, it seemed that activity was everywhere. Fledgling birds of all types left their nests and tried their wings for the first time. Adult birds were feeding their young on the multitude of insects and on the abundance of fruits and plants that had blessed the earth. Warm summer rains fell, bringing new life to the land of the woodland lakes; and flowers of all shapes, sizes, and colors sprang up from the earth. On sunny hillsides, red and yellow columbines hung from their stems, their fragrant flowers waiting for bees and hummingbirds to drink their nectar. Near the streams and in the low meadows were Turk's-cap lilies and Indian paintbrush, with their yellow upper leaves and their brilliantly colored red-orange flowers. In shady spots grew yellow lady's-slippers and fringed gentians, whose bright-blue, bell-shaped flowers were just beginning to bloom.

The wolf pups grew larger each day, and so did their appetites! By the time they were 10 weeks old, their diet consisted entirely of meat. Even amidst this land of plenty, the four pups and their parents were rapidly depleting the game in their hunting area. Old White and his mate knew that the way of wolves was to travel, for to remain permanently in one area was to starve. So the wolf family left the den on the hillside and began searching for a new hunting ground.

The pups were excited about the move at first; but before the night was over, they longed to be back in their den. They were not aware of it, but from now on they would be sleeping on the open ground. The adjustment came quickly, however, and soon all thoughts of the den were forgotten.

For the remainder of the summer, the four wolf pups spent most of their waking hours hunting—sometimes with their parents, and sometimes by themselves. The summer was drawing to an end when two of the young wolves—Greedy and Mischief—inadvertently scared a mink into the lake while they were searching for a hare that had escaped them. The two pups would continue their search for some time before finally giving up on the hare and settling for some frogs and mice.

Part II

Autumn

SUMMER FADED INTO AUTUMN, AND, AS THE NEW SEASON arrived, changes came over the woodland. The three words that best described the land were *abundance, activity,* and *color.*

Autumn was truly a time of abundance. Great quantities of fruits, nuts, seeds, and grain were ready to be eaten and harvested. Acorns, butternuts, and hickory nuts hung ripe in the trees, or lay on the ground beneath. Gray squirrels gathered them ceaselessly. With nervous energy and reckless abandon, they carried the nuts and seeds one at a time and then dropped them in tiny holes in the ground, burying each one separately, just below the surface. The squirrels *appeared* to be storing food for the cold weather ahead. But they would quickly forget where most of the seeds lay buried, so that their efforts would accomplish little more than to plant new trees for future forests.

Meanwhile, the industrious little chipmunks, mice, and gophers were storing food in their dens and burrows, so that they would have enough to eat during the long winter months. Birds, bears, and deer also ate heavily of the nuts and seeds. Rabbits, bears, raccoons, and other animals feasted on the fruits and berries, while blackbirds, ducks, and geese devoured the wild rice that grew in the lakes.

The lakes were bordered by a profusion of colors. Red came first to the leaves of the sumacs, and next to the grapevines. Black ash and butternut leaves turned dull yellow and then loosened and fell to the ground. The clear yellows of the birches and elms came soon after, followed by the gold of the hickories. The deep wines of the red oaks were preceded by the flame of the soft maples and by the widely ranging colors of the hard maples. Amid this brilliant display of autumn colors, the pines and spruces still held their deep, dark green. These evergreens would, as their very name suggested, keep their green leaves throughout the year, outlasting the gaily colored oaks and maples that now made them look so drab by comparison.

Autumn brought little change for the great horned owl. His hunting and feeding habits were about the same now as they had been throughout the summer. One thing he did not like about the fall season was the shrill, noisy cawing of the crows. The birds gathered into large flocks in anticipation of their migration south, and they traveled about in boisterous bands that irritated the owl, making him feel very uneasy.

One night he spotted some of the crows roosting in a tree, and he snatched one of them up as it slept. It was a young crow from the previous spring that was now fully grown. The owl seized it in such a way that the crow could offer no resistance other than a short squawk before it succumbed. Its cry alerted the other crows to the danger. But with eyes made only for daylight, they were unable to fight the owl, and he got away.

The next morning the flock of crows took off in search of their attacker. With daylight, the situation was more in their favor, for they could see well in the bright light whereas the sunshine was not to the owl's liking. The crows hunted throughout the day without success. Then, just as the sun touched the treetops, one of them spotted the quarry in a

Norway pine thicket. A cry of alarm brought the others, and, had it not been that darkness was approaching, they surely would have vanquished the owl. Two things contributed to his survival. Because the great horned owl had better daylight vision than most other kinds of owls, he was able to fight off his attackers for a while. The crows, on the other hand, were wary of the approaching darkness, when the advantage would swing back to the owl. So they soon broke off their attack and sought refuge for the night, hoping that they might hunt the owl down the next morning.

That night the owl found the crows again and killed two of them. Before daylight came, he wisely flew several miles away and hid in the thickest part of three closely growing spruce trees. He slept very little that day as he waited fearfully for the hunting crows. They did not find him, and he avoided them that night. But he was very tired from a day without sleep, and also very hungry.

Two weeks later the crows moved out of the owl's area, and his home again became a silent wilderness. Keeping his cavernous stomach full was once more his prime concern—that, and his never-ending campaign to eliminate the elusive mink.

The mink spent his time much as the owl did, hunting to keep meat on his menu and playing a hide-and-seek game with his feathered competitor. He was a furry bundle of nervous energy that was almost constantly on the go.

THE AUTUMN WAS ALSO A BUSY TIME FOR THE THREE- LEGGED muskrat, who tried to keep one step ahead of her old enemy the mink. One night after the mink and a cottontail had passed by the cone-shaped house of weeds that she was building for the winter, the muskrat made her way back to the shore, swimming over the glasslike surface of the lake. It was early evening, and the colored splendor of the shoreline was mirrored in the lake and accented by the vivid pink of the setting sun. The colors did not appear striking to the muskrat, however, for her eyes were designed to see the world only in black and white.

When she reached the site of the mounded weeds, the muskrat smelled the strong, unmistakable odor of the mink. But knowing that it had left the area, she went about the task of finishing her house. She approached the house from under the water, and with her sharp incisors, she chewed out an entrance from the bottom. She continued digging at it until she had hollowed out a room a few inches above the water. The material that she removed was piled on top to thicken the walls. She made a second room, connected by a very short passageway from the first room, and from it she dug a second exit that led back down into the water. It was late in the night before she finished the excavating, and she was very weary.

In the three days that followed, the muskrat dug another tunnel in the muck, from beneath the house out into the lake. With this tunnel, she could enter and leave her house even when the lake was covered over with thickly frozen ice. At the end of the third day, the tunnel was finished; but the job had been tedious, and her arthritis was causing the muskrat much discomfort. She spent a good while cleaning and grooming herself, carefully smoothing her fur and even removing the dirt from between her toes. Then she settled into the smaller of the two rooms to sleep. The room was just large enough to accommodate her, and, lying in the small enclosure, she soon became warm and comfortable.

The muskrat was just beginning to doze off when she heard a slight noise outside her house. Alarmed by it, she quietly slipped through the tunnel and swam out into the lake. Her quick action proved to be very wise, for at almost the same instant that she had left the house, a mink had entered it through the other entrance. The muskrat swam far out before surfacing, and then lay motionless on the water, floating amid the rice stalks. She did not swim back to her house for a long time. She feared the mink more than she feared most other enemies, and she was not about to risk being ambushed by him in her own home.

As autumn wore on, the muskrat continued to pile more weeds, rice stalks, cattails, and reeds on top of the house, always with a bit of mud to bind it together, so that the house became higher and wider, and its walls thicker and stronger. Finally the day came in November when a layer of ice covered most of the lake, with only a few open areas remaining. Along with many other muskrats that inhabited the lake, the three-legged muskrat took advantage of the ice, sitting on it at the edge of the open water. She used the resting spot as a convenient launch pad from which she dived into the lake to gather underwater weeds. She always returned to the platform of ice to eat the weeds, for she did not care to eat without having her feet on something solid, and she did not feel like swimming all the way back to her house.

Soon the lake was entirely frozen over except for the place where the small river entered. The muskrat made a hole through the ice by paddling vigorously in one spot just underneath it so that the water motion would melt the ice away. Then she brought mouthfuls of weeds to the hole and gradually built a protective dome over it, with a small room inside. The one-room structure was located almost a hundred yards out into the lake. The muskrat would bring under-water plants here to eat during the long winter ahead, using the crude shelter as a feeding house.

Snows eventually came and covered both the feeding house and the larger cone-shaped house of mud and weeds. But for the muskrat, the snow was no problem: it helped to insulate her against the numbing cold, and it reduced the frequency with which she had to swim in and out óf the entrances to keep them from freezing solid. Until the warmth of spring would thaw away the ice and snow, the muskrat would remain sealed beneath them, a willing prisoner of her underwater world.

To THE COTTONTAIL, AUTUMN DID NOT BRING ANY SPECIAL problems. He did, however, adopt several new homes. Within the small area of land where he roamed, he found four suitable resting places, each of which was as much home to him as the others were. He chose them mainly for the purpose of concealment, so that when he rested and slept, he could not be seen from the air or from the ground.

The oldest of these sanctuaries was the fern patch, which the rabbit still used occasionally. Another consisted of two small balsam trees that grew close together, with boughs that reached to the ground. A thick clump of speckled alders with an umbrella-shaped top was another; and a windfall where a large aspen tree had fallen and taken two small birches with it served as the cottontail's fourth home.

From each of these homes, the cottontail had several avenues of escape. Although he was always prepared to bolt out at high speed if necessary, the rabbit preferred to sit quietly and allow the danger to pass by if possible. He had interconnecting trails leading from one home to another, and numerous trails that led him out to where he foraged for food. Never a week passed that he did not have at least one close brush with death, but still he survived. The approach of winter did not concern the cottontail, for he was as ready for winter as he would ever be, living each day as it came.

THE YOUNG WOODCHUCK LITERALLY ATE HIS WAY THROUGH summer and into autumn. For a long time, he remained near the burrow in which he had been born, continuing to use the underground home as a place for safety, shelter, and sleep. But, like his brothers and sisters, he made many long trips away from it. Eventually the day came when he did not return to the burrow, something within him telling him that it was time to go out on his own.

For several days the groundhog wandered about, homeless. He searched through and inspected many of the holes and underground tunnels that he came to, but none of them satisfied him. Being without a place of refuge gave the woodchuck an uncomfortable feeling. He remembered his terrifying encounters with owls, foxes, and other predators, and he feared that one of them would pop out of nowhere and strike without warning. One day the young woodchuck was forced to climb a tree when a wolf cub was closely pursuing him. Until then, he had not even known that he could climb; but with the wolf close behind him and with no place to duck into, the woodchuck had instinctively gone up the tree. He had climbed it with surprising ease, but had gone only to the first large branch, where he patiently sat until the young wolf gave up on him and left.

This newly found method of escape from ground-dwelling predators gave the woodchuck a greater feeling of security as he traveled about. He was almost always within a short run of a tree, and yet he still longed for the safety of an underground home like the one he had left. Eventually he found an area where he wanted to live. It was a place where sparsely growing trees allowed much sunlight to reach the earth, so that many of the weeds and plants that the woodchuck liked covered the ground. A tiny creek bubbled through the area, and not far away was a lake; thus the woodchuck would always have plenty of drinking water. But the area's

greatest attraction was a gently sloping hillside composed mostly of gravel. When the woodchuck surveyed it, he knew at once that it would make a perfect site for his home.

Early the next morning, he began digging a burrow in the side of the hill. For the entrance, he chose a spot between two large roots of a pine stump. He made the entrance wide enough so that he could easily race through it, or even turn around in it to view the world behind him. He slanted it down steeply for a few feet, and then began digging a narrower, nearly level tunnel.

The woodchuck used the sharp claws of his front feet to loosen the dirt. Then, with his three-inch hind feet and his powerful hind legs, he scraped and kicked the dirt behind him. Backing slowly while he kicked, he would work a pile of dirt out of the entrance; then he would dig farther in and push the next pile of dirt out the hole. Two rooms he made for himself, each one large enough to sleep in, and both of them a foot higher than the tunnel so that they would remain dry in case of flooding. Twenty-five feet from the entrance, the woodchuck slanted the tunnel up to daylight for a second exit. He was careful not to kick any dirt out of this hole. Instead, he removed the dirt by pushing and scraping it back through the entire length of the tunnel, all the way to the main entrance, where he kicked the dirt out past the pine stump.

He made no attempt to conceal the large mound of dirt that he had thrown out the main entrance. He merely spread the dirt out in a wider but flatter mound that clearly marked the den. The other entrance was a different matter, however. Not a bit of fresh dirt betrayed the spot; the woodchuck had purposely brought the tunnel up inside a small briar patch so that it would be well hidden. Here, in this secret entrance, he could sit up on his haunches and view the surrounding countryside, his coat blending in with the briars and the brown weeds that grew among them. One narrow trail led through the briars, away from the hidden entrance, but the woodchuck used this passageway only when necessary.

With the addition of some dry grass and some soft milkweed down to the bedrooms, the woodchuck's new home was ready for winter. All the animal needed now was a thick layer of body fat to help keep him alive while he slept through the long winter ahead. Working toward that end was more pleasure than work, for eating was the woodchuck's favorite pastime.

He had eaten his first full meal after finishing his home, and was heading toward the creek for a drink of water, when an insect buzzed over him. It circled back and buzzed past his head. For some reason, the woodchuck panicked and attempted to run for cover. But the swiftly flying, loudly buzzing insect could not be avoided. The tormentor was a female botfly, an extremely harmful type of fly that looked and sounded like a small bumblebee. Suddenly it darted in and laid a tiny egg on one of the woodchuck's forepaws.

Twice more the botfly dove in, each time attaching another egg to a forepaw. Then the fly, satisfied with its accomplishment, moved on in search of other victims.

Once the pesky botfly had buzzed out of sight, the woodchuck continued on toward the creek. He stepped into the cool water, drank his fill, and then sat on the bank of the creek to groom himself. Two of the three botfly eggs had been rubbed off in the grass or washed off in the water, but the woodchuck transferred the third egg from his forepaw to his lower lip as he cleaned himself. The egg hatched within a few minutes, and a tiny wormlike larva emerged. The larva immediately began burrowing into the woodchuck's soft lip, causing some swelling and a great deal of itching there. The woodchuck rubbed his lip with his paws, and even scratched the lip against the bark of a tree for relief. In the meantime, the larva continued to burrow until it had gone all the way through the lip and into the mouth. Soon after that, it was swallowed into the woodchuck's stomach. Stimulated by the digestive juices in the stomach, the botfly larva clung to the stomach lining. Then, after absorbing some of the juices and taking a short rest, it began burrowing through the stomach lining. It continued burrowing very slowly, feeding on the woodchuck's body fluids and growing as it went.

A parasite, the botfly larva would remain inside the woodchuck as it developed and grew. Many months would pass before it would finally leave the woodchuck's body. It would live off of and destroy the woodchuck's body tissues, causing the host a great deal of harm and pain. But as yet the botfly larva was very tiny, and the discomfort that it caused the woodchuck was only minor. Certainly, it did not dull the woodchuck's enormous appetite for clover, alfalfa, and weeds!

One day while he was busily filling his stomach, the groundhog spotted an animal that he had never seen before.

70

About two feet long, it had a wide, flat body that was built very close to the ground, with short, thick legs. A narrow white stripe ran between its eyes and on down the middle of its back; this, together with the white markings on its cheeks, gave the animal a striking facial appearance that it wore like a badge. It had a waddling sort of gait as it moved along the ground, and the long, powerful claws on its forefeet looked like they were made for digging. The woodchuck did not recognize this animal from sight, and its scent was unfamiliar to him; so he wisely remained hidden. He had learned the danger of owls, foxes, wolves, and wildcats; but, to him, this badger was a new and totally unpredictable kind of predator from which *anything* might be expected.

As the woodchuck watched, the badger began digging at the entrance to a chipmunk's burrow. The sharp-clawed animal was indeed a fast and powerful digger. The dirt flew behind it, and soon the badger had nearly disappeared underground. Seeing the opportunity for a disappearing act of his own, the woodchuck scampered toward home while the badger buried its head in the hole.

To THE WOODCHUCK, THE BADGER WAS SOMETHING TO BE avoided. But to the little chipmunk that huddled in the underground burrow, the excavating badger was an enemy intent on invading his home and devouring him. As the badger dug deeper into the tunnel, the chipmunk watched his entire summer's work being destroyed. The badger had already reached the chipmunk's first storeroom, where a pile of acorns and a mound of chokecherry seeds were carefully stored for the cold months ahead. The chipmunk watched the provisions being plundered and buried, and then retreated farther into his underground refuge.

Although he was less than four months old, the chipmunk

was fully grown and was living completely on his own. Just two months ago, he had been in his mother's home, along with his brothers and sisters. He had played and tumbled with them, running, frolicking, and wrestling in a way that had developed his strong muscles and his sharp reflexes, preparing him for the day when he would go out into the world alone. Two weeks later the frisky little chipmunk had reached maturity. He was about eight inches long, including his tail, with strong hind legs and small, delicate feet. Like his mother, the reddish-brown rodent was marked with black and tan stripes on his face, back, and sides.

Following the urge to go out into the free, wind-swept world, the chipmunk had left home. From then on, he was ruled by three necessities of life: food, shelter, and escape from predators and death. (A fourth natural drive, that of reproduction, would not affect him this season.) There was also a great curiosity to satisfy—holes to be investigated, trees to be climbed, new foods to be tried, and new lands to be visited. Finding food was not much of a problem during this fruitful time of the year. For although the chipmunk's appetite was large, the variety of foods that he liked was also large, so that the chipmunk could always find something to ease his hunger. The small, striped rodent feasted on nuts, berries, and seeds of all kinds, as well as on grasses, flowers, and mushrooms. For added protein, he would not turn down an insect, a small frog, or even an unguarded bird's egg.

A few days after leaving home, the chipmunk started digging his underground burrow. He began it in an area of tall grass, scooping the dirt out and throwing it behind him. The tunnel went almost straight down for the first two feet and then slanted more gradually for several feet until it reached a depth where frost would not penetrate. From there, the chipmunk dug horizontally for many more feet, making the tunnel just wide enough to accommodate him but too narrow for most of the predators that would seek his flesh. Then he began carving out the storage rooms, three in all, where food would be kept for the long winter. The fourth room, dug slightly higher than the tunnel and the other rooms as a precaution against flooding, would serve as the chipmunk's sleeping quarters.

Still laboring strenuously in deep darkness, the chipmunk continued the tunnel onward and upward. He moved all the soil out of the original entrance, several yards away, so that when a second exit finally opened toward the outside world, not a trace of dirt marked the spot. Only a small hole was there, hidden by a bit of vegetation. When a third exit had finally been completed, the industrious little worker turned his attention to the original entrance hole. Lest any sign of his burrow remain there, he must dispose of the mound of dirt that he had thrown out. Wisely, he pushed as much of the dirt as he could back into the hole, sealing off the first entrance. The remainder he carried away, scraped, and scattered, so that no sign showed that he had ever excavated at all. The underground burrow now had only two entrances, both concealed by vegetation and neither showing a trace of piled soil.

After finishing his new home, the chipmunk began filling the underground pantries with food for the winter. He obtained the first of his provisions from a nearby oak tree. The acorns were not yet falling by themselves; so the little rodent scurried up the tree and ran out onto its branches, where he snipped off the acorns with his sharp front teeth, letting them fall to the ground. Then he raced back down the tree to gather the acorns up. He wisely chewed off their sharp points before packing the nuts into his cheek pouches and carrying them to his burrow.

The food-gathering trips took up most of the chipmunk's waking hours. Often, the shriek of a hawk or the yap of a

fox would cause the striped rodent to freeze or to race for cover. In each case, however, he quickly forgot about the danger and went back to the job of storing up nuts for the winter. Acorns and chokecherry seeds filled the first of the chipmunk's food compartments. Into the second went hickory nuts and the seeds of wild pea vines. The third and last compartment was filled with a variety of foods, including dried fruits and the seeds of grasses.

Upon entering his burrow one day, the little chipmunk had made the mistake of allowing an approaching badger to see him disappear into the hole. The badger was built low and broad, looking more like a small tank than a real animal. Digging rodents out of the ground was his specialty, and he headed straight for the chipmunk's burrow. The dirt flew behind him as his powerful legs scooped it out. Within a moment he had dug in half the length of his 30-inch body, and in another moment he was all underground. Still he continued to dig. He reached the chipmunk's first storage room, and then the food flew behind him and was buried.

Deep in the burrow, the chipmunk huddled in fear. He saw his narrow tunnel being enlarged to huge proportions. He saw his first two storerooms being destroyed and his food being buried. And then he saw the deadly fangs and ferocious head of the digging badger.

In panic, the chipmunk ran up to the other exit and peered out the small hole as the badger dug on, past the third storeroom and into the chipmunk's sleeping quarters. The chipmunk was afraid of running out into the open with such a deadly predator around, but he knew that he could no longer remain in the burrow. Everything was gone, destroyed, buried, and soon the badger would reach him. The chipmunk raced out of the exit. But the badger, suspecting what the chipmunk was up to, had backed out of the other hole himself. A short footrace resulted, with the chipmunk barely making it to the safety of a small elm tree. He climbed to the very top, and the badger, who had labored so hard for nothing, ambled on.

The chipmunk huddled in the tree the rest of the afternoon, and on until midnight, when the cold finally drove him down. He found shelter under a pile of leaves and remained there for the rest of the night. Late the next morning, after the sun came out and warmed things up, the chipmunk began moving about, looking for something to eat.

Although he could not really think, he somehow was aware of the seriousness of his problem. His home had been destroyed, and, even worse, his winter's provisions were gone. It was much too late for him to rebuild his home and replenish his supplies, for hibernation time was nearly upon him.

He sneaked along, nosing into every hold and depression, searching for a home, for a place to stop and relax. He found a white oak acorn partially buried in some soft leaf mold, and he carried it under the curve of a large rock. Hidden there, he ate the succulent nut, enjoying every morsel. He traveled on, along the edge of a narrow meadow, and on a small knoll he came to a hole in the ground very similar to the one he had previously lived in. Around it was the smell of chipmunk. He entered the hole, and the odor of chipmunk was strong and fresh. One was surely living here, and he knew that it would not welcome him—any more than he would have welcomed another chipmunk into his burrow. He had worked very hard to harvest enough food to carry him through the cold winter, and he would not have considered sharing it.

He hesitated for a while, just inside the hole. Then, though he knew it was unwise, he started down the tunnel. He stopped when he heard the sound of the owner coming up to drive him out. Then he turned and ran, making such a quick exit that the burrow's owner never saw him.

It was getting very late in the afternoon. As the sun dropped below the treetops, the little striped rodent became more concerned about finding shelter. He had never liked being about after dark. The weather was colder than it had been the previous night, and the chipmunk now was desperately searching for a warm place to spend the night. He scampered along a fallen log, and on one end of it found an opening just large enough to accept his small body. He crawled inside, pressing himself as far from the opening as possible. In that position he spent the entire night, becoming more chilled as each hour went by. With the arrival of daylight, he was almost too cold to move. When he crawled out into the cold morning air, hunched and shivering, his muscles stiff and unresponsive, he felt very weary and ill at ease. Two days earlier, he had possessed everything he needed; now, he had nothing.

He moved on, searching for the safety and security of a

home like the one he had lost. He stumbled onto the shriveled remains of a wild plum and ate most of it. Then, only a short distance away, he came to the entrance of an underground burrow. When he entered the inviting-looking hole, he detected not the smell of chipmunk but, rather, the scent of another small animal, a scent that he had detected several times before. The odor was neither strong nor fresh, however, and this led the chipmunk to believe that the burrow's owner was not now within.

Secure in this thought, the chipmunk went deep into the burrow. He soon came to a large storeroom filled with acorns, hickory nuts, and wild plum pits. Two feet farther on was a second room, this one filled mostly with pincherry pits and the seeds of wild barley. Grass-lined sleeping quarters and a second exit completed the underground home. The chipmunk knew that there was almost no chance that he could remain here, in this burrow, unless he was willing to fight its rightful owner for it. Yet he was so tired—and his other options were so bleak—that he curled up on the bed of grass and spent the night there, catching up on all the sleep he had missed.

The chipmunk had no way of knowing that the burrow's owner, a 13-lined ground squirrel, had fallen prey to a red-shouldered hawk three days ago. But when several days had passed and the chipmunk still had not been driven out of the burrow, he guessed that its original occupant was gone for good and would never return to claim the burrow. Thus the beleaguered little chipmunk fell heir to a well-made, well-stocked home—all that he needed to see him through the coming winter.

A WEEK HAD PASSED SINCE THE WOODCHUCK HAD FIRST SEEN the badger. During that time the parasitic botfly larva living inside the woodchuck's stomach had continued chewing and burrowing through the muscles and fat tissues that it encountered. The destruction and discomfort caused by the burrowing invader was not great, however, for the larva was still very small. But suddenly the woodchuck had a very large, highly destructive invader to worry about. For the *same badger* that he had seen digging at the chipmunk's burrow was now tearing away at the entrance to his own home!

Luckily for the woodchuck, the badger was temporarily stymied in its efforts: the large, immovable roots of the pine stump on either side of the entrance were much too close together for the badger to squeeze its wide body through. But the digger did not give up easily. Suspecting that there was another entrance to the woodchuck's home, the badger searched and smelled about until it located the camouflaged hole. Then, with great zeal, the badger began digging its way in. The woodchuck panicked, for he knew that his secret escape route had been discovered, and he thought that his burrow was being invaded from both ends.

The frightened woodchuck cowered in the deepest part of the tunnel, afraid to stay and afraid to leave. He did not know if only one badger was outside, moving from one hole to the other, or if there were two badgers, each digging at a different site. Nor did the woodchuck know how fast his adversary could run. The woodchuck was not far from a tree, which he could easily climb, but he was not aware that the badger's claws were designed only for digging and could not grip a tree.

The woodchuck was on the verge of dashing out of the burrow and making a run for it when he realized that the invader was no longer making any progress. The badger had reached a spot where the woodchuck had tunneled between two rocks. They were too large and heavy for the badger to move, and its body was too broad to slip between them. So the badger had no possible way of reaching the woodchuck. As on the day when it had dug for the chipmunk, the badger had done a good deal of work for nothing.

Although the danger had passed, the woodchuck was so paralyzed with fear that he did not leave his battered burrow for a long time. He remained there the rest of the day, all through the night, and well into the second day. In spite of his great hunger, he stayed beneath the ground. But if the groundhog was going without food, the parasitic larva within him was not. It continued to feed greedily with its sharp barbed mouth, shredding the tissue so that it could be swallowed and digested, all the while heading toward its final resting place in the host's body.

When the woodchuck finally emerged from the burrow, he spent the rest of the day gorging himself on nearby vegetation. He spent most of the next day repairing the damage that had been done to his home. The burrow would never be camouflaged as well as it had been before; but, aside from that, no permanent harm had been done to it.

Finally the day came when the temperature dropped to a point that signaled an end to the woodchuck's feeding. He crawled into his underground home and packed in a bit of hay to plug the tunnel on each side. It was not enough to block off the air entirely, but just enough to keep the draft out. This done, the woodchuck curled up in a large pile of grass and settled into a deep sleep.

By MID- AUTUMN, THE WOLF PUPS HAD GROWN ENOUGH FOR the family to hunt together as a group. They were now nearly as large as their mother, though not nearly so big as Old White. By their first birthday, the young wolves would be almost full grown, weighing close to 75 pounds, and they would be masters of the forest.

This was the mating season for deer, moose, and other large ruminants, and they could often be seen wandering about, searching and calling for mates. The wolf pups were not yet big enough or strong enough to hunt these animals. Instead, they preyed on smaller game such as mice, rabbits, squirrels, and other rodents. These animals were easy to catch now, with no snow cover on the ground. But in a few weeks, with the onset of winter, they would become much scarcer, so that the wolves would be forced to hunt larger animals.

The pups' first encounter with a moose was a startling and exciting one. The family of six had started out on a hunt when there was yet an hour of daylight left. With Old White in the lead, they skirted a swamp, passed silently over a hill of thick willow growth, and traveled with the wind along a narrow strip between two lakes. At the same instant that they caught its scent, they heard and saw a monstrous beast come crashing toward them from out of the spruces. The attacker made fierce snorting noises as it charged ahead.

It was a huge animal with a ridiculous-looking head, wide antlers, and flying hoofs. The wolves immediately scattered in every direction. Two of the pups came within inches of the attacker's flying feet, but both escaped unharmed.

The six hunters quickly reassembled and moved on. The pups were too frightened to want anything more to do with the fearsome beast. And Old White, quick and powerful as he was, knew better than to attempt to bring down a healthy bull moose—not unless there was a deep, crusted snow to slow down those deadly, hard-kicking hoofs.

THE BRILLIANTLY COLORED LEAVES OF AUTUMN FADED SLOWLY to shades of brown, and then loosened and drifted to the earth, their descent hastened by wind and rain. The forest became a cluster of barren trunks and branches, the tops pointing skyward like lonely church spires. The exceptions were the evergreen trees, and some of the red oaks whose drab brown leaves clung stubbornly to the branches, rustling faintly in the breeze.

The warm, sunny days of Indian summer passed on, and by late autumn the forest had become a bleak-appearing world. The days grew colder until one still night most of the lakes froze over. Within a short while, all water that did not flow became solidly icebound.

Then the day of the first snow arrived. It began in early afternoon with small flakes fluttering slowly down to the earth. They melted and vanished in an instant, with the only result being the wetting of the leaves that covered the ground. As the snow continued to come down, bits of white began to appear on the fringes of the fallen leaves, creating a mottling of brown and white on the forest floor. By night-fall, the entire ground was white. Winter had descended on the land of the woodland lakes.

Part III

Winter

THE SNOW HAD CEASED BEFORE MORNING, BUT DAYLIGHT showed a five-inch covering of it on the ground. For many of the animals in the land of the woodland lakes, this snow-covered world was one that they had never experienced before. Hundreds of footprints appeared in the blanket of white, including those of the cottontail. Although the young male rabbit had never seen snow before, he was not greatly alarmed by the new sight. He continued to hop and feed as usual.

The cottontail's main danger lay in the change of background color. Whereas his gray-brown fur had previously blended in well with earth, grass, and leaves, it now stood out in sharp contrast to the light-colored landscape. To escape predators, the cottontail would have to be even more cautious than he had been before.

The mink had lived through the previous winter; so the sight of the falling white crystals had not been new to him this time. His tracks appeared along the shores of the lakes and up to the edge of an open river, where he often plunged in to find a meal beneath the surface. Fish, frogs, crayfish, and muskrats made up the bulk of his diet.

The snow served as a seeing aid for the great horned owl. This is because most of the creatures that he preyed on— rabbits, squirrels, mice—were much easier to detect against the background of white. One animal that he fed on, however, had a clever way of overcoming this problem. The varying hare, or snowshoe rabbit as it is called, changed its fur from brown in summer to white in winter so that it would blend in with its surroundings. With the hare already wearing its winter coat, the new white snow was a blessing. Yet the all-seeing eyes of the great horned owl were often able to detect even the movement of white on white.

The snow had little effect on the chipmunk or the woodchuck, other than to help insulate their homes. Neither animal had yet gone into total hibernation, though the woodchuck had almost reached that point. The botfly larva was continuing to chew its way through his body, growing larger as it went. By now, it had become a grotesque-looking maggot. It was causing the woodchuck a good deal of discomfort, as were the fleas that lived in his fur and dined on his blood.

THE SNOW ALSO PROVIDED ADDITIONAL INSULATION FOR THE three-legged muskrat, both in her home and in her small, one-room feeding house, or feeder. While reducing the heat loss, the snow also reduced the amount of sunlight that came through the ice, but the muskrat's eyes were still capable of seeing well.

One of the chores in the muskrat's underwater world was to prevent too thick a layer of ice from forming on the water surface at the entrances to her home and feeder. If the ice should become too solid, the muskrat would not be able to break through it and she would be doomed. She made the hundred-yard trip out to the feeder several times a day. After clearing the single entrance of any ice, she would make an excursion along the lake bottom to gather weeds. Then she would return to the feeder, where she would leisurely enjoy the tasty vegetation she had gathered.

Life in her closed-in world soon became very routine. The

underwater swims would have been a simple task for the muskrat had it not been for the disabling stiffness that had entered her hips. The gradual spreading of the arthritis into her hips had been a severe blow, for it was her powerful rear leg muscles that she needed to use in propelling herself through the water. Her right hip was particularly sore, and when she swam out to the feeder, she put most of her effort into the left leg to reduce the pain. At first the muskrat managed to keep her food-gathering trips short by limiting herself to the waterweeds that grew around the feeder. But as the weeks went by, her food-gathering trips became longer and longer, though there was still an ample amount of food within swimming distance to easily see the muskrat through the winter.

By mid-January, the ice on the lake was well over two feet thick, with as much snow covering the ice. Although it was confining, the ice offered many advantages to the muskrat. For now there was no danger of hurtling hawks or swooping owls. The ice kept out many other predators, too; and, best of all, it served as a barrier against the dreaded mink. Living beneath the ice as she did, the muskrat knew nothing of the snowstorms or the blizzards with howling winds that raged just above her. In her house, the temperature remained nearly constant; and in the water, her fur—made waterproof by a special oil—kept her dry. Sealed off from the wind, the water of the lake remained almost motionless, its slight movement detectable only by the gentle swaying of slender waterweeds.

As her arthritis worsened, the muskrat began making only two trips to the feeder each day instead of the usual three or four. She cut back on all physical activity, spending most of her time curled up asleep in the smaller of her home's two rooms.

One day when the weather was particularly cold outside

and when the muskrat had waited longer than usual before returning to her feeder, she was unable to break through the ice that blocked the entrance hole. She pawed at the water below it to melt away the ice; but with her breath running out, she still was unable to break through. The entrance was frozen solid, and the hundred-yard swim back home would be impossible for the muskrat without another lungful of fresh air.

In desperation, the muskrat pressed her nose up to the ice and expelled her breath against the undersurface. Her exhaled air remained there in a large bubble, and in a short while, she breathed the rejuvenated air back in. With her lungs full of oxygen, she started back home. Halfway there, she was again forced to expel her breath in a large bubble against the ice and then to wait a short time before sucking it back in. This strange game of oxygen economy kept the muskrat alive, enabling her to make it safely back home.

Having lost the use of her feeder and the food that grew around it, the muskrat now had to rely solely on the food that she could find and gather on a two-way trip from home. Because of her arthritis and her age, she was no longer the powerful swimmer she had once been. She made only short sorties out under the ice, and the food within her limited swimming range was rapidly depleted. No longer could she find any weeds above the lake bottom. The roots of water-lilies and wild rice, which she dug in the mud to obtain, were the only items left on her menu.

In early autumn, the muskrat had weighed close to three pounds. On February 1, she weighed barely two pounds, having lost almost a third of her body weight. Had she been in good health and able to swim as usual, the old female muskrat could have survived the winter with little difficulty. But her health was not good, and her growing inability to gather food was now a serious threat to her life.

BEFORE THE DEEP SNOWS OF WINTER CAME, A STRANGE animal had moved into the forest. It walked tall on two legs, and it carried things in its hands. The intruder moved into an abandoned log cabin along the bank of a small river, and it spent most of its nights there. During the day, it set out metal traps that caught and held minks, foxes, and other fur-bearing creatures. The two-legged animal skinned the hapless victims and saved their furs. Even more frightening, it carried a long metal stick that made a loud noise and that killed deer, moose, and other large animals from a distance.

The wolves feared very few creatures of the forest, but they soon learned to fear this strange and deadly intruder, this man. So that they might avoid him and the terrible stick he carried, Old White and his family traveled mostly at night, when the darkness would help conceal them from the enemy's view.

The nights grew colder and the snow deeper; but the wolves, with their thick, heavy coats, were ready for the wintry weather. Storms blew in from the west, and the whistling wind drove the white crystals into deep drifts. When squirrels, mice, and other small animals began living beneath the snow in order to avoid their enemies, the wolves were forced to turn to larger animals for food. The family of six rapidly developed into a smoothly operating, highly efficient wolf pack—a team whose members would remain together, hunting and traveling as a single unit, for a long time.

A large herd of white-tailed deer had been moving along the edge of the forest in search of food for several days. It was a clear night when the wolves spotted the game for the first time. The herd had split into two groups, and it was the smaller group that the wolves encountered. At the sight of the wolves, the frantic deer turned and ran in headlong flight, moving with long, powerful strides in a tight formation with no stragglers. Old White quickly gave up the chase, for he knew that it would be almost impossible for him to overtake the swift-footed prey. Years ago he had run tirelessly for many miles at a time; but now, in his twelfth year, Old White no longer had the stamina or endurance of the younger wolves, though he could still match them in brute strength. In a short run, he would be out in front; but in a long chase, he would grow lame from old injuries such as the terrible blow his shoulder had taken from the hoof of a thousand-pound moose, or the near-fatal goring his chest had taken from the horns of an angry buck.

Later that night, as they traveled quietly over the top of a small ridge, the wolves spotted the larger group of deer lying in some bushes at the edge of a meadow. As the wolves advanced on them, the deer rose and turned to run. One old buck was slow to rise, however, and he hesitated another moment before fleeing. This slight hesitation sealed the male deer's fate. For his sluggish response told Old White and the other wolves that the buck was weak and tired—and this meant that he could be caught.

The slow-moving buck was easily overtaken, the wolves drawing alongside him before he was halfway across the meadow. The end was violent but quick. In killing the tired old deer, the wolves had saved him from suffering a slow and painful death brought on by starvation and cold. At the same time, they had provided themselves with a fresh supply of meat that would help sustain them for several days.

THROUGHOUT THE WINTER, THE GREAT HORNED OWL SPENT more time than usual doing battle with other birds of prey that dared to hunt in his part of the forest. With food scarcer and more difficult to procure in winter, the owl had to eliminate as much of the competition as possible. He drove off a red-tailed hawk soon after the first snowfall; and a few days later, he attacked a barred owl that was almost as large as he was, sending the trespasser on its way. The following evening he heard the harsh, rasping cry of a saw-whet owl, a very small owl measuring only eight inches from head to tail. In this case, the great horned owl did not drive the intruder away. Instead, he made a meal of the bird, tearing it apart before eating it.

Of the creatures that the great horned owl normally ate in summer, many were no longer available. While muskrats were sealed beneath the snow and ice for the rest of the season, woodchucks, gophers, and chipmunks were hibernating beneath the ground. Most of the small woodland birds that the owl found tasty had gone south for the winter, leaving the owl and other large birds of prey behind. So the owl was existing mostly on mice, shrews, squirrels, and rabbits. But even many of these were becoming scarce. Their numbers had dwindled greatly since the peak population period of early summer. What is more, mice and shrews were living mostly beneath the snow, where they could not be seen, while weasels and snowshoe rabbits were wearing their white coats, which blended in with the winter landscape.

To overcome these obstacles, the great horned owl relied on his highly developed senses of sight and hearing. His eyes were able to pick up very slight movements at great distances, and his hearing was marvelous indeed. The owl's ear openings were shaped and designed in such a way that they enabled him to pinpoint the direction of any sound and to determine just how far away it was. This proved very helpful to the owl in tracking down animals that were hard to detect against the snow.

The owl obtained many mice by concentrating his efforts around clumps of grass and weeds and around the bases of trees, where the wind pattern often left a dished-out area of snow along one side. On still days, the sun would melt the snow in these places as the sunlight was absorbed by the dark vegetation, so that the ground was actually bare in some spots. Swarms of mice came to these places to feed on the seeds of the grass and weeds, and with them came shrews and weasels to feed on the mice.

These animals made up the bulk of the owl's conquests. He often dived in and picked up a mouse as it burrowed along just under the snow, leaving behind a small ridge as it moved. This method of hunting brought the owl many misses, however, and even when it was successful, the catch was a very small one. For a four-pound bird with the capacity to digest nearly his own weight in food every day, the owl required a lot of mice to keep himself going. It was the winter food supply, more than anything else, that limited the number of owls in the land of the woodland lakes.

In mid-January the first major blizzard of the season struck. The great horned owl waited it out in a dense grove of evergreens, protected from the wind as well as he could be. He remained perched on a sturdy branch very close to the trunk, where the wind would not sway the branch and where the trunk would help block the wind. The owl's feet remained firmly clamped to the branch, and with his body sitting low, his feet were engulfed in his feathers. Fortunately, the owl was wearing many more feathers now than he had worn during the summer.

For three days, as the relentless wind and snow continued, the owl remained perched in the tree. He was a wise enough bird to know that hunting would be useless so long as the storm raged. For a deep cover of new snow lay over the ground, and nearly all the other creatures of the woodland were doing just as the owl was—hiding and waiting.

When the storm finally blew itself out after the third day, the owl was in such a weakened state that he could barely summon up the energy to fly. Yet fly he must, for he could not live one more day without food. Starvation was averted when a gray squirrel came within easy reach of the owl. It was a food that he seldom got, because the squirrel was most active during the daytime whereas the owl hunted mostly at night. A good period of hunting followed the storm. Although most of the mice remained buried deep beneath the snow, hordes of other creatures that had been inactive during the storm were now out looking for food. The great horned owl made a feast of the animals, and his strength soon returned to him.

In late January an uneasiness came over the owl. He began making long flights over his land without making any attempt at hunting. He would occasionally stop during the flights to perch high in a treetop, where he would make extended hooting calls. After nearly a year of solitude, the great horned owl was once more experiencing the need for a mate.

When he failed to find a female that he could court, the owl began extending his flights far outside his own realm.

On one of these trips, he came upon a female of his own species. But she was already with another male, and she was unresponsive to him. Indeed, both she and her mate resented his intrusion. The male was almost as big as he was, and the female was even larger. So when they threatened to attack him, he wisely retreated to his homeland.

The cool reception did not dull the urge that drove him on, however; and in the days that followed, the great horned owl continued to make similar trips into other lands.

INSIDE HIS COZY DEN, THE WOODCHUCK SLEPT SOUNDLY. IT was a much deeper sleep than he had ever known before, for he was now in a state of true hibernation. His body temperature, which normally hovered around 100 degrees, now ranged between 38 and 40—only slightly above freezing; and his heartbeat, which only a month ago had averaged about a hundred beats a minute, was now down to just four or five. The slumbering groundhog took only one shallow breath every few minutes, so that he gave the appearance of being more dead than alive.

In this state of complete dormancy, the woodchuck was using the energy that he had stored up as body fat as slowly as possible. When he had entered his burrow for the last time in late autumn, the woodchuck had weighed almost 12 pounds, with a half-inch layer of fat covering his entire body. Although much of this fat had already been burned up, there was still enough of it left to keep the hibernating groundhog alive until spring.

February 2, Groundhog Day, came and went, but this particular groundhog was completely unaware of it, with no thoughts of attempting to peek outside at the weather. In fact, he had no thoughts at all. The badger that had hunted him in the fall was no threat to him now, because it, too, was

in a hibernating state, though its sleep was not so deep as the woodchuck's.

As the woodchuck slept, oblivious to everything, the botfly larva continued to feed and grow inside his dormant body. By this time, the larva had chewed its way to its final resting place, just under the skin in the middle of the woodchuck's back, where the woodchuck would not be able to reach easily with his mouth or paws. The skin was raised in a large lump where the ugly maggot lay. Behind the larva, in the path where it had moved, the host's body was busy repairing the damage to its tissues. With only one of the parasites inside him, the woodchuck had an excellent chance of surviving the damage that it caused. But if the woodchuck had been infested with a large number of the parasites, his life would have been in jeopardy.

The botfly larva would remain inside the woodchuck's body, growing and developing, for several more months. With the arrival of spring, when the woodchuck would come out of hibernation and emerge from his den, the wormlike parasite would at last leave the woodchuck's body by chewing through the skin and dropping to the ground. It would spend up to 10 weeks in the ground, during which time it would develop into an adult botfly complete with legs and wings. Then, if it survived the birds and other creatures that preyed on it, the fly would lay some of its several hundred eggs on the legs or lips of another unsuspecting victim like the woodchuck. Thus would the cycle be completed, with the botfly continuing not only its species but also the misery and harm that it dealt out to others.

Although the woodchuck would not be free of the parasitic botfly larva for quite some time, one of this other parasitic problems had already been solved by his hibernation. For the fleas that lived in his fur and that fed on his blood were forced into dormancy by the near-freezing temperature of his body. Not until spring, when warmth and activity returned to the woodchuck's body, would the fleas again become a problem.

One of the most interesting things about the sleeping woodchuck was that he had a closed system in regard to water. He did not swallow a drop of water all winter. Nor did he expel any liquid from his body. A tiny bit of moisture was, of course, being lost through his lungs from his infrequent exhaling. But this loss was compensated for by the trace of water being produced from the oxidation of the hydrogen in his body fat. Thus there was no danger of the woodchuck's becoming dehydrated during his long winter's sleep.

Unaware of the amazing functions his body was performing, the hibernating woodchuck slept on, his sleep not to end until his eventual reawakening in spring.

Not far from the slumbering woodchuck, the chipmunk was confined in a similar den. He slept for days at a time, but unlike the woodchuck, he did not go into total hibernation. His body remained much warmer than the woodchuck's, and he woke occasionally to feed from his supply of nuts and seeds. After satisfying his need for food, he usually went up to the burrow's opening and swallowed a few bites of snow to satisfy his need for water. Then he would tidy up the burrow a bit and go back to sleep.

The little chipmunk had been very fortunate in finding this underground haven with its grass-lined sleeping quarters and its food-filled storage rooms. For without it, he would not have lived for long. On one cold, windy day in February when the temperature dropped below zero, the chipmunk settled back into his cozy bed of dry grass and leaves. As he positioned himself on the bed, some fleas hopped from the grass onto him, and some from him onto the grass. He scratched and rubbed with one foot and then another to ease the uncomfortable feeling that the bloodsucking pests gave him. Then he groomed himself, carefully smoothing back his fur before lying down for another long sleep.

It was several days before he woke again. He was groggy at first, but eventually he roused and stretched himself. A short while later, he began making his way through the tunnel. The darkness was complete, with not a trace of light to show the way. But even though the chipmunk could see nothing, he knew the tunnel so well that he could walk through it without the slightest hesitation, his sensitive whiskers serving as feelers to mark the tunnel walls as he moved along.

The chipmunk stopped at the first storage room that he came to. He dined on some wild barley seeds, chewing them leisurely, for time was of little importance in this world of total confinement. The chipmunk's supply of nuts and seeds was more than half gone; but the winter was half gone, too, and the chipmunk had lost very little weight. Of course he had very little to lose, for he had not stored up any extra body fat for the winter as the woodchuck had.

Having consumed a number of barley seeds and a couple of pincherry pits, the chipmunk made his way up to the burrow's exit to get a "drink" of solid snow. Three feet of snow covered the hole, but a tiny bit of diffused light shone through the thick white wall. His occasional trips up to this snow-covered exit were the only times when the chipmunk was able to see even a trickle of light.

After getting his fill of snow, the little chipmunk went back down to his sleeping quarters. His five and a half months of solitary confinement was passing well for him. He cleaned and groomed himself in the darkness and then slipped back into the deep sleep that would continue intermittently until spring.

IN CONTRAST TO THE CONFINEMENT THAT WINTER BROUGHT TO the muskrat, the woodchuck, and the chipmunk, was the increased freedom and maneuverability that it brought to the cottontail. For although he stayed within the bounds of his home range, rarely venturing outside it, the cottontail was now able to hop on and across the solid, ice-covered surfaces of lakes and ponds, rivers and streams. This saved him a lot of time in getting from one place to another, and it gave him access to areas that he had been unable to reach by land.

So the cottontail—unlike the woodchuck and other hibernators—was just as active now as he had been during the summer and fall, and his life-style was little changed. It consisted mainly of eating, of avoiding those who would eat him, and of traveling over and about his area of land, his piece of real estate. Although he was less than a year old, the cottontail was a full-grown rabbit weighing almost three pounds. He had not begun the winter with any excess fat, however. The added weight would have reduced his speed and agility; and if he was to stay out of the claws and jaws of his pursuers, he must remain trim and fit and light of foot. This was especially true now, in the midst of winter, when his gray-brown fur stood out against the white landscape, making him all the more visible—and all the more vulnerable to attack!

The cottontail soon learned just how big a disadvantage the white background was to him. His "education" began one day when a red-tailed hawk spotted him while he was moving along in some tall grass. This was a situation in which the cottontail would have been perfectly safe before the snow fell, when his fur would have blended in with the grass and weeds, hiding him from the hawk. As it happened, the cottontail escaped the winged predator by the smallest of margins, diving into a tangle of brush just ahead of the bird's swishing talons.

Later that day the same scene was reenacted, with the rabbit narrowly escaping by bolting into a clump of evergreens only an inch ahead of the hawk's weapatoned feet. Then, as darkness fell upon the land, the weary little cottontail caught sight of yet another bird of prey, one that he had encountered many times before, the great horned owl. But this time, the owl was not after him. It was after the *hawk*, which had invaded its territory. The owl attacked the trespasser and drove it out of the area, thus eliminating one of the cottontail's most relentless pursuers.

When he was not dodging hawks, owls, and other predators, the cottontail spent his time eating. The snow covered most of the green leafy plants that he had feasted on throughout the summer and fall, but food was still

plentiful. Of course, the rabbit's diet was considerably less varied than before. He was now limited mostly to twigs, bark, buds, and the fruit of bushes and trees. The rabbit did not consider this a hardship, however, and he knew which shrubs and bushes tasted best. His favorite variety was red osier, a shrubby dogwood with dark-red branches. Several other shrubs he considered almost as tasty: hazel, aspen, basswood, and sumac. Raspberry canes were also to his liking, and he dined on them often.

A few days after the first snow had fallen, a warm day came, and the snow became wet and sticky. When the cotton-tail hopped around in it, the snow clung to the hairy pads of his feet. He stopped every so often to bite the accumulated snow from his feet, even picking it from between his toes. The built-up snow felt uncomfortable to him. What is more, it was a hazard; for it slowed the rabbit down, and he knew that to stay alive he must remain speedy. He stopped traveling any more that day, remaining hidden and motionless until the coolness of night hardened the snow again. The following day, several more inches of it fell.

On the night after the snowfall, the cottontail spent most of the dark hours feeding and hopping about from one bush or shrub to the next. Just before daybreak, he headed back to his makeshift home under the fallen aspen and birch trees. He was about to enter it when a 35-pound lynx suddenly leaped at him from ambush. The big cat had discovered the rabbit's shelter and had waited there for hours for the unsuspecting occupant to return. The cottontail escaped the lynx by dashing straight underneath the leaping attacker and by bounding away in an erratic zigzag run through some thickly growing spruce trees. After a number of clever dodging maneuvers, he finally threw the lynx off his track. He then lay in hiding—motionless except for his twitching nose—until he was sure that the cat had given up the chase and had moved on in search of other prey.

Three days after his brush with the lynx, the cottontail discovered a large aspen tree that had been blown over during the last snowstorm. A large portion of the treetop was within his reach, and it was like a banquet for him. He feasted on the tender buds, and on the smooth green bark of the smaller limbs and twigs. During the next week he came back to the tree over and over again, feeding on it for a while each night. The snow around the tree eventually became packed and trampled from the rabbit's broad hind feet.

Although eating was his main fulfillment in life, the cottontail also enjoyed traveling over the several acres of land that made up his home range. He explored every inch of his domain, and he often darted through the bushes and shrubs for the sheer joy of it—an activity that kept his leg muscles in excellent condition. When leaping across the snow in great bounds, he left behind the distinctive trail of the swift-footed rabbit, with his large hind feet landing ahead of his front feet, so that his tracks made it look as if he had been running backward.

In mid-January, when a blizzard hit, the rabbit holed up in his home under a thick clump of speckled alders. He remained there for the entire three days of the storm, allowing the snow to drift over him and cover him. He had no food — and no means of getting any. But he kept a small hole open so that he could stick his head out and satisfy his need for water, eating just enough snow to quench his thirst.

When at last the storm subsided, he emerged from the shelter with just one goal in mind: to satisfy his now-ravenous appetite. To his delight, he found that food was more readily available now than it had been before the storm. For with the added height of the snow to walk on, he could obtain twigs and berries that were previously beyond his reach. Each new snowfall brought the cottontail up to a new level — and a new supply of food. In one place where the wind had blown the snow into a particularly high drift, the rabbit dined on the tops of a clump of sumac, even sampling the cone-shaped clusters of red fruit. This was a real treat for him, and he enjoyed it immensely.

By the time February arrived, the cottontail was in excellent condition, stronger and healthier than ever. He had already beaten the odds, for of the young cottontails born the previous summer, only about one in six was still alive. The little cottontail had been very lucky so far. But his luck must hold out; he must live through the remaining days and nights of winter if he was ever to produce any offspring. For although he was now old enough to mate, it was still too early in the year for that, with the mating season some two months away.

One day during the second week of February, the cottontail was hopping along in the snow, getting his fill of food and fresh air. It was a warm and peaceful day, and large flakes of snow were slowly drifting down through the still air. Without any warning, he felt the searing pain of an owl's talons slicing into his back. He kicked and twisted as hard as he could. One of the owl's feet had been brought to bear, but the other one was hanging limp, apparently maimed and useless. The cottontail struggled desperately to free himself of the owl's grip. If the talons of both the owl's feet had penetrated him, the rabbit would have had no hope of escaping. But with the owl using only one foot, the battle was a near-standoff. Suddenly a large, four-footed animal came rushing toward the great horned owl. The owl's talons immediately relaxed their hold on the cottontail, and the victim tore free. But before the rabbit could reach safety, he was seized by the powerful jaws of the four-footed animal, and from this predator there was no escape.

THE FREEZING OVER OF THE LAKES DID NOT GREATLY ALTER the life of the mink. He was an animal of the water's edge, and not even the sealing off of the water could change that. He continued to patrol the shorelines of the rivers and lakes, traveling along in small bounds when he was not stopping to snoop. In the moonlight he flowed across the white snow, blacker than the darkest shadows, the possessor of limitless energy, the embodiment of wild freedom.

Except in extremely cold weather, there were spots of open water in the rivers wherever the water flow was rapid, giving the mink many places to enter and leave the water. From these open spots he would swim beneath the ice for considerable distances in search of food. Beneath the ice were fish, and embedded in the mud for the winter were frogs and crayfish, which the mink dug up and ate. From the water, he found tunnels that led up into the riverbanks; and at the ends of the tunnels, he found the dens of muskrats, the mainstay of his winter diet.

Not only did the rivers afford him avenues to the water, but the lakes and marshes did as well. There were places beneath the insulating snow where flowing springs kept away the ice. The mink had an uncanny ability for discovering these routes into the lakes. Sometimes he detected them by smell, or by the looks of the snow that covered them; but more often, he simply remembered having been there before. Generally, though, the swamps and marshes were more likely to afford him accessibility than the lakes were. Protected from the cold by layers of grass and moss covered with snow, some spots in the marshes remained completely unfrozen.

It was in a boggy area covered with peat moss that the mink now made his way through the surface into a muskrat runway. The two muskrats that he found in the den at the end of the tunnel each weighed as much as he did, but he took them both with ease. He stayed in the den that night and for most of the next day, alternately sleeping and gorging himself on the muskrat meat.

He left after dark to travel on, moving in powerful bounds over the deep snow. With each leap, he sank more than the length of his short legs into the soft snow, but it did not slow him perceptibly. His supple body nearly doubled up with each jump as it coiled to stretch for the next leap, the hind feet landing exactly in the prints that the front feet had just left, so that the mink's tracks showed only two prints instead of four. The mink made many miles that night along lakes and the river and through the woods, poking his nose into holes and climbing trees to investigate nests and hollows. Just before daybreak, he returned to the same muskrat den he had left. He had not worried about food during his night's prowling, because he had known there was still some meat left in the den. Before he departed again, the muskrat meat was all cleaned up.

The temperature had been dropping steadily for the past two days, and it now was many degrees below zero. It was the cold, more than the snow or anything else, that affected the mink's ability to find the meat he needed to continue life. The cold did not prevent the mink from spending time in the outdoor air, for he was clothed in a warm, perfectly fitting mink coat—one that covered every portion of his body, including his feet. What the cold did do, however, was to block the mink's entrances to the water, where most of his food was to be found. The river was frozen solid, so that not even the fast-running spots were open; and nearly all the mink's entrances to the lakes and marshes were closed, as well. To eat, the mink must find food from other sources.

Leaving the frozen lakes and rivers behind, the mink moved into the forest, where he changed his mode of traveling by sliding down the wooded hills. It was something he enjoyed, and he never missed an opportunity to do so whenever the hill was steep enough and the snow conditions were right. He had only to spread out his feet and slide down the hill on his slippery belly fur.

At the foot of a hill, near a clump of weeds, he discovered a shrew that had just killed a mouse, and the two tiny animals both became his. The shrew he ate on the spot, but he carried the mouse under a bush before consuming it. (Whenever possible, he preferred to be in or under some sort of shelter when he ate.) Two hours later, he stopped below a large red oak tree. The snow around the base of the tree was packed from the activity of squirrels, and the gnawed shells of acorns were scattered about. Peering up the tree, the mink found what he was looking for. In a fork halfway up the tree was a round squirrel's nest, constructed mostly of leaves.

Up the tree the mink went, as nimbly as the squirrels themselves, directly to the nest. There was a single gray squirrel inside, and being a daytime animal that never ventured out in the dark, it was asleep. The mink squeezed through the opening on the side of the nest and quickly secured his meal. After eating more than half the meat, he lay down beside the remains of the squirrel and went to sleep, staying in the warm nest until the arrival of darkness the next evening. Then, after finishing what was left of the squirrel, he ran out onto the tree. He did not travel straight down to the ground, but ran across and leaped through the branches of several trees before finally descending the smooth trunk of a hickory.

The mink always found it more difficult to obtain food when he was forced to hunt away from the water, and such was the case tonight. He spent the entire night searching and finding nothing. When dawn came, he crawled into a hollow tree and slept awhile. But hunger roused him before long, and he began hunting again before noon.

Although he usually hunted at night, the mink was not reluctant to be out in the daytime. There were a few meat-eating animals that he had to watch out for, but most of them were creatures of the night just as he was. There was a great horned owl in the area that had made several tries for him, and once he had come so close to where a bobcat crouched that it had lunged at him. But the mink's quickness and agility had saved him from these enemies. Foxes and wolves were his enemies, too, but he could climb trees, and they could not; he could swim swiftly beneath the ice, and they could not; he could squeeze into small holes, and they could not. All things considered, the mink was very well equipped for survival. He knew enough to be wary of bobcats, lynxes, and other large predators, and yet the mink was not really aware that he would ever die.

In late afternoon, while moving through a grove of jack pines, he spotted a red squirrel in a tree. It was busily extracting the small seeds from a pine cone. The squirrel suddenly gazed down and saw him, and immediately it fled. The mink in turn raced up the tree and attempted to follow the squirrel through the treetops. He was a good climber; but the mink was no match for the squirrel, and he soon gave up, with the squirrel escaping and hiding.

The mink was very weary by now. The hunt of all night and most of the day, climaxed by his futile pursuit of the squirrel, had taken a heavy toll on him. So he found a cozy hollow in a tree and curled up in it for a rest.

Later that evening the mink returned to a lake and began prowling along the south and east sides, where the wind had blown the snow into deep drifts along the shore. He traveled mostly beneath the snow, burrowing his way along at ground level and only occasionally coming up to the surface. In three hour's time, he had worked his way half the distance around the lake; and in all that way, he had not found so much as a single mouse or shrew.

This was the longest the mink had gone without food

during the entire winter. He was weak and tired, but his hunger pushed him on. Thinking that he might have overlooked something, he reversed his direction and headed back over the same area he had just covered.

TWICE A DAY, THE OLD FEMALE MUSKRAT MADE SHORT TRIPS under the ice, digging roots out of the mud and bringing them back to her house to eat. What little food she could gather on her trips to the lake bottom was not nearly enough to keep her alive. So, to supplement the scanty meals, she began feeding on the inside of her house! Being constructed of various plants and weeds, the house was not only edible but also nourishing. The muskrat was somewhat reluctant about consuming the home that she had labored so long on, but she had very little choice in the matter. It would be many weeks yet before the warmth of spring would melt away the snow and ice, freeing her from her confinement. She must survive until she could move about freely and eat of the abundant vegetation, when the sun's warmth would ease the pain and stiffness in her body.

She began by nibbling at the walls and ceiling of the larger room. She rationed her feeding carefully, so that at first the difference in her house was hardly noticeable. But as the walls and ceiling grew thinner, the room grew larger and the house cooler. The other room of the house was still only slightly larger than she was, and the muskrat spent most of her time there in an effort to stay warm. To conserve her strength and energy, she allowed the underwater exit leading from the larger room to freeze over, so that she was left with only one exit. She ate as much of the large room's ceiling as she could reach, and she ate through the room's walls until she got down to the snow and ice. Finally, she was forced to start nibbling at the smaller room. As its walls became thinner, with more ice and snow exposed, staying warm became more and more of a problem for the muskrat.

The old muskrat had survived many ordeals—the loss of her foot, the loss of her children, the repeated attacks of minks and other enemies. But now her plight seemed hopeless. For if she did not freeze to death, she would surely die of starvation. Or so it seemed.

It was a bitterly cold night, and the muskrat had not eaten for days. But the cold and hunger had a pleasant numbing effect on her, so that she was experiencing little pain or discomfort. Her only desire was to sleep. She had just settled down and closed her eyes when a mink entered her house. With the other exit frozen solid, she was trapped. She made a gallant effort to defend herself, but in her weakened condition, she did not have a chance. Her long and painful struggle for survival had come to an end.

WHEN THE MINK LEFT THE MUSKRAT'S HOUSE, HE HEADED straight across the lake. He was moving into a slight wind, which gave him the advantage of being able to detect the scent of any animal in his path long before he actually came upon it. A half-moon gave just a trace of light as it shone through a thin layer of clouds.

Suddenly the mink felt the sting of talons piercing his side, and instantly he whirled to defend himself. A great horned owl had approached him from behind, and the wind had kept a sound from reaching him. The owl's left foot had grasped the unsuspecting mink just behind the shoulders, and the talons of the right foot had settled into the neck.

The great horned owl had always found such a firm hold to be unbreakable, but he had never had a *mink* in his grip before. Squealing with rage, the frenzied prey twisted and squirmed like a bundle of steel springs. The owl lost his grip

111

on the mink's neck; and, hissing and snarling, the mink sunk his long, pointed teeth into the bird's right leg. In the struggle, the talons on the owl's left foot dug deeper into the mink's side and back while the mink's teeth ripped into the bird's leg again and again. The owl tried to release his hold on the savage fighter, but he could not. Just then a deep-sinking talon pierced the mink's heart, and the victim went limp.

The owl had won largely because he had caught the mink off guard with his sneak attack from the rear. But to the winged hunter, it was a victory that had been won at great cost. For the owl's right leg had been mangled in the struggle, and it was now completely useless. With much difficulty, the owl took off from the lake in awkward flight, leaving the mink lying in the blood-splattered snow—a carcass to be claimed and picked clean by scavengers, many of whom the mink had once stalked.

The owl flew directly to his hideaway in the Norway pine tree. Once there, he positioned himself close enough to the trunk so that he could rest one shoulder against it. Although the maimed bird remained in this comfortable position through the next day, he got very little sleep. He managed to perform his regular chores that evening, but the movement required for expelling the pellets of waste material from his body caused the owl much pain and discomfort.

He was very hungry by the following evening, but he was still too weak for hunting. He remained in the pine tree for three days, getting as much rest and sleep as he could. Then, on the third night, his nagging hunger finally forced the owl to look for food. He flew slowly over the lakes and woods, looking for anything but finding nothing. A long time passed, and finally he managed to pick up a deer mouse with his good foot; but the tiny rodent did little to quell his hunger. The owl was about to fly back to the Norway pine when he saw a cottontail up ahead of him, hopping along in the snow. It was moving at a leisurely pace, and in an open area that had few shrubs or bushes to jump into.

Only the most desperate and compelling hunger could prompt the maimed bird to try for a frisky, hard-kicking animal like the rabbit, but try he must. He swooped down from behind and got a good grip on the prey with his left foot. The rabbit reacted violently, and the owl, in his weakened condition, was hard pressed to hang on to it. Suddenly he saw a large, four-footed animal come rushing toward him. He let go of the rabbit to make a quick getaway, but he was too late. He managed to get a weaponed foot in the face of the charging attacker, ripping its nose and tearing a gash near its eye; but the owl was no match for the powerful young wolf, and the contest was over in a flash.

In the end, it was the owl's disastrous battle with the mink that had proved to be his undoing. For if he had not been maimed, the great horned owl might easily have escaped the inexperienced young wolf. As it turned out, though, the winged hunter had fallen prey to a hunter more powerful than he, and the land of the woodland lakes had lost one of its most majestic and commanding creatures of the sky.

THE TIRED OLD DEER HAD BEEN THE LAST GOOD CATCH FOR the family of wolves in some time. All the other large game animals in the area appeared to be strong and healthy, and the six wolves could not succeed in taking any of them. The few moose that they approached either stood defiantly, ready to fight, or ran away with such speed that the wolves never got close enough to attack them.

The wolves returned to the remains of the deer for several nights, until virtually every bone had been stripped of its flesh. The pressure to find more food was greater on Greedy,

with his keen appetite, than on the rest. One night he went alone to the site of the deer kill, hoping to find one last tidbit that the others had overlooked. But when he got there, the wolf found that the carcass had been claimed by a wolverine, which attacked Greedy on sight and sent him scurrying.

This was too much for Greedy. The deer belonged to *him*, and he was not about to be driven away from it by this insolent wolverine, a stocky meat-eating animal smaller than Greedy was. The wolf doubled back and charged the wolverine. But instead of fleeing, as Greedy had thought it would, the wolverine whirled around and cut a three-inch slash in Greedy's shoulder. The injured wolf quickly retreated—and this time he did not return.

The powerful wolverine was a shaggy-furred, foul-smelling creature with sharp teeth, short legs, and strong claws. It was a loner that had wandered far south of its normal Canadian haunts. A member of the weasel family and an oversized relative of the mink, the wolverine was 40 pounds of savage fury that feared nothing and that attacked anything. Although Greedy was unaware of it, running away from one of these fierce fighters was nothing to be ashamed of, for a wolverine would not hesitate to attack even a full-grown bear; and more often than not, the bear would yield to it!

His pride injured, his shoulder slashed, and his stomach emptier than before, Greedy headed back to his family. Near the center of a lake, he came across the lifeless body of a mink; and though it was frozen solid, he consumed it quickly. With his hunger appeased for the moment, Greedy moved on. It started to snow just as he reached the shoreline. The wolf climbed atop a small hill and then froze, for he saw a cottontail moving straight toward him. He waited anxiously as the prey drew nearer, ready to pounce on it when it came within reach. The rabbit was only a short distance away when Greedy saw a great horned owl drop out of the sky and attack the furry-tailed animal. The bird clasped the rabbit tightly with one foot while the other one hung limp and useless. A highly spirited victim, the cottontail squealed and fought as the maimed attacker tried desperately to hang on to it.

Greedy, seeing his prospective dinner being taken away, rushed downhill to attack the owl. The big bird immediately released the rabbit and stabbed at Greedy, ripping his nose and tearing a gash near his eye. But with one crunch of the wolf's powerful jaws, the owl was crushed. Greedy dropped the bird and went after the cottontail, overtaking the wounded rabbit with ease. So what had started out as a disastrous night for him had ultimately provided Greedy with a meal of a mink, an owl, and a rabbit. The gluttonous young wolf had paid a price for the feast, what with the wounds he had received from the wolverine and the owl. Yet his stomach was full, and that was all that mattered to him.

ONE NIGHT WHILE GREEDY AND THE OTHER FIVE WOLVES were trudging through the snow, they picked up the scent of meat along the bank of the river. Moments later they discovered a large hunk of red meat lying in the snow. Old White detected another scent, very faint, and he growled a warning. The other wolves pulled to a stop. All except Greedy, who could think of only one thing—*food.* He charged at the hunk of meat and began tearing it apart. As he did so, the strange scent that Old White had detected earlier became stronger; and Old White, growling louder than before, retreated several jumps. Greedy started to run, too, but he managed only a few jumps before he suddenly slowed, staggered, and fell on his side, convulsing in the snow as his muscles stiffened from strychnine poisoning. The wolf's muscles contracted tightly, and his own sharp teeth pierced through his protruding tongue as blood spurted from his mouth. His back arched and stiffened. His lungs went into a spasm and then stopped, choking the life from his body. It was all over in a matter of minutes.

The wolves had learned to hunt only at night in order to avoid being seen by the tall, two-legged animal who carried the stick which made a loud noise and which killed from a distance. But that clever foe had tricked them; he had killed Greedy not with the stick but with a different weapon—one that was far less visible than the gun, but just as deadly. It was too late for Greedy. But with his death, the other wolves learned to be extremely wary of meat that lay temptingly in the snow—theirs for the taking—especially when it smelled of something more than meat.

Early the next morning, the wolverine that had fought Greedy for the deer carcass passed by the wolf's frozen body, the back arched stiffly in the agonies of death. Nearby, the wolverine found a piece of meat in the snow. After eating part of it, the stricken animal staggered through the forest, snarling and snapping at the pain in its stomach. The wolverine had consumed as much of the meat—and as much of the strychnine—as the wolf had. Yet the wolverine's strong resistance to poison would allow the animal to survive, though not without first suffering a great deal of excruciating pain and misery.

GREEDY WAS GONE, BUT LIFE WENT ON AS USUAL FOR THE five remaining wolves. They spent most of their time looking for sick or injured deer and moose that they could overtake without much trouble. Although the frustrated hunters were having very little success, their luck was soon to change. For the huge bull moose that had attacked the wolves the previous fall, terrifying them as he charged from ambush, was back in the wolves' hunting territory; and he was suffering from a crippling disease that made him more vulnerable to his enemies every day.

The moose had caught the disease in late autumn, when one of his front feet had become infected with a parasitic fungus. Days later, when the moose made his sneak attack on the wolves, the infection was so slight that the wolves were unaware of it. But during the days and months that followed, the infection had worsened steadily. As the diseased hoof cracked and blistered, it became more and more painful to walk on; and with each step he took, the moose left behind a drop of pus in his tracks. The pus contained more of the disease-causing fungus, which could be passed on to infect the hoofs of other moose, elk, or deer if they should happen to step on it—now, or even in spring, after the snow had melted.

The wolves passed near the bull moose one night while they were scouting around for big game. Seeing that he was alone, they pressed him to test his speed and strength. The moment they realized that he was limping, the battle was on. The moose was angry and defiant. Roaring his challenge, he charged the closest of the wolves as they circled him. He put up a good fight, though with his crippled leg he was slower and less forceful than before. Old White waited for the right moment and then darted in from the rear several times. His sharp teeth sank into the moose's left hind leg, biting and chewing until the leg was incapacitated. With only two good legs left to stand on, the big bull moose was helpless against the wolves as they tightened the circle around him and charged from all sides. They all went down together, amid flailing hoofs and flying snow. Once the victim was down, the end came quickly. The fallen moose would spread no more of the disease-causing fungus to infect and cripple other hoofed animals.

One of nature's intended roles for the wolves had been demonstrated: the killing of sick animals to prevent the spreading of disease. In addition to eliminating diseased animals such as the moose, who had endangered the health of his entire herd, the wolves did a good job of weeding out the slow and the dull witted, the weak and the injured. By singling these animals out and eliminating them, Old White and his pack were keeping the herd strong by ridding it of its weakest members. Of course, the wolves were not doing this intentionally; they were merely feeding themselves. But since slow, weak, and sick animals were easier to catch than healthy ones, these were the game that the wolves hunted most often—and with the most success.

Greedy's death had taught the wolves never to eat the funny-smelling pieces of meat they found lying in the snow, and they traveled mostly at night to escape the gun of the tall, two-legged animal who lived in the cabin. But that deadly enemy had one more lesson for them. Mischief stepped onto a trap one night and yelped in pain as the steel jaws closed on one of his front feet. He was alone that night, and he fought the trap for hours, snarling and biting at the metal jaws and then jerking and pulling against the chain. The pain in his mangled foot was excruciating; yet he strained and pulled on it in a frenzied effort to free himself.

When daylight came, Mischief grew more panicky, and his efforts to free himself became more frantic. His desperate twisting and pulling finally broke the wire that fastened the chain to a stake. With the heavy steel trap still gripping his foot like a vise, he hobbled away through the deep snow —and none too soon, for just behind him came the trapper! Limping and struggling, the wolf continued on as best he could, and yet he gained very little distance on the trapper. Occasionally he would stop to rest, to ease the pain in his foot, but never for very long, because his pursuer was never far behind.

Mischief went down a hill and across a ravine. He was climbing the hill on the other side when he felt a sudden, searing pain tear through one of his hind legs. At the same instant he heard the loud noise that could come only from that terrible stick the two-legged animal carried. The stricken wolf tumbled over and rolled to the bottom of the hill. With great effort, he righted himself and began dragging himself back up the hill. A second shot slammed into a nearby tree as Mischief shuddered in fear. The next shot entered his brain; and the moment it did, the pain in his hind leg and front foot ceased. Mischief would never feel pain again.

In LATE FEBRUARY, STORMS DESCENDED ON THE FOREST WITH great fury. The snow swirled about in blinding clouds of white, and the wind blew the flakes into deep drifts. After each storm the sky would clear, and the temperature would plummet to 30 or more degrees below zero.

The wolves could not travel in daylight for fear of the gun; they could not eat the hunks of meat they found for fear of the poison; and they dared not go where they smelled the scent of the trapper or the odor of steel for fear of a trap.

The tall, two-legged animal in the cabin wanted more wolves. If they would not take his bait or go near his traps, he would simply have to be more resourceful. He hung a large kettle of water over the fire and put some traps in it. Then he cut some pieces of willow, alder, and spruce bark and dropped them into the boiling water. This, he knew, would cover the odor of steel and human, so that the wolves would smell nothing but the natural scents of the wood. He also soaked his leather mittens in the bark juices; and from then on, he handled the traps only with those mittens.

One night after a fresh snow had fallen, Howler was hunting along the bank of a river when he picked up a familiar scent. Moments later he saw the lifeless body of a rabbit lying in the snow, just a few yards ahead of him. He circled the rabbit twice and then cautiously approached it, sniffing its scent as he moved closer. He seemed to detect another odor besides the rabbit's, but it was so faint that he was not really sure it was even there.

Rather than go straight for the rabbit, Howler moved toward a hillock a few feet away. He climbed it so that he could look the area over, as Old White had taught him to do whenever he was suspicious of something. As he stepped on top of the mound, he heard and felt the sudden thud of steel jaws closing on his foot. The trapper had known how suspicious the wolves might be of his bait; so when he set the trap at the meat, he also set one of his de-scented traps at the highest point of ground nearby. The plan had worked beautifully, with Howler stepping right into the steel trap that lay hidden atop the hillock.

The temperature dropped to 25 degrees below zero that night, and by morning it had dropped another 10 degrees. Howler lay on top of his injured foot to keep it from freezing. In the severe cold, the small river below the bank on which he lay froze over completely, where previously the rushing water had kept it open. All day long, as he waited for the dreaded two-legged animal to come, Howler alternately struggled at the metal trap and lay atop his throbbing, twisted foot to keep it warm.

When darkness came, he was still trapped on the bank of the river, with no other animal in sight. The weather began to warm slightly that night and still more the next day. But Howler couldn't stop shivering; and by nightfall of the second day, he was very sick and weak, with his foot badly swollen and his energy almost drained. He fell into a fitful but much-needed sleep that night. Then, early on the morning of the third day, he awoke with a start. Panic gripped him as he opened his eyes and saw the tall, two-legged animal walking along the opposite bank of the river.

Howler leaped to his feet and lunged against the trap. The trapper saw him struggling and then hurried across the river, rushing over the layer of ice that had formed during the recent cold spell. He was running hard now, unmindful of the thin ice, and he was carrying that long, terrible stick in his hand.

Summoning up all the power and strength within him, Howler made one final, desperate lunge for freedom. Suddenly he found himself tumbling over in the snow; and before he could get to his feet, he heard a loud, piercing scream. As he looked up, he saw the two-legged animal breaking through the ice and going under the rushing water. Howler lay there, motionless, watching the hole in the ice and expecting to see the trapper emerge from it at any moment. But it never happened. Minutes went by, and the two-legged animal did not appear. All that remained of him was his stick, which lay on the ice alongside the hole.

When at last he got to his feet, Howler looked down at his injured foot in amazement. It was free! He had been so spellbound by the trapper's scream and by seeing him go through the ice that he had not even noticed that his foot had come free in that last, desperate lunge he had taken.

Slowly and painfully, Howler made his way to a thick clump of spruce trees where the dense branches had caught the snow to form a roof with a cozy hollow beneath it. Here the wolf licked and nursed his injured foot. Fortunately, no bones had been broken, though the foot was badly swollen and cut. The weather was calm and warm that day, with the temperature climbing to 35 degrees above zero by mid-afternoon. As the snow began to melt, a portion of the white roof above him came trickling down on Howler.

For three days he lay there, under the spruces. His foot began to heal, but starvation was drawing dangerously close. On the fourth day he moved out along the riverbank,

where the sun had reduced the snow cover, and began working his way upstream. He caught two mice while poking along in the snow, and he gulped them down greedily. The mice did little to ease the wolf's hunger, however.

Howler spent most of the next day sleeping under a large windfall. Then, soon after darkness came, he heard a familiar sound in the distance. It was the sound of the chase; a pack of wolves was on the trail of a large animal. Later that night Howler came to the remains of a freshly killed deer. He knew at once that this was the work of Old White and the others; there was no mistaking those scents. Howler ate his fill of the meat and then lay down to rest and to wait, for he knew that they would be back.

Suddenly an urge came over him. Ever since he had stepped in the trap, he had been too dazed and sick even to think about howling. Now he raised his head and sent a loud howl out into the night. From not too far away, the howls of three wolves came back to him, and he settled down to wait. Howler was home.

A Word from the Author

The stories about the animals in this book are, of course, fiction, but they are realistic in regard to the type of life and the actions of each particular species involved. It is my wish that these interwoven accounts of the forest and its creatures might help to show the reader what life is like for some of our animal neighbors and what the world looks like from their vantage point.

I also hope that this book might help to get more people interested in nature, because I feel that those who enjoy nature and who learn about it will be more willing to help protect it. At the same time, they will be enriching their lives in one of the best possible ways.

It is heartening to know that in the last few years there has been a large increase in the number of people who are students of nature. One statistic that I read recently shows that there are now 10 times as many birdwatchers and people who feed birds as there are hunters—and the ratio is increasing. I think this is a good sign.

I am not suggesting that no one should hunt. But there is not room for many more hunters; and, fortunately, there are many other ways for most of us to enjoy nature, such as hiking, camping, canoeing, snowshoeing, birdwatching, and wildlife photography. Each of these activities holds forth the possibility of a richer life, and most of them can be done at very little expense.

Nature is deeply imbedded in us because we are creatures

of the forest and plains. We came out of the woods to build villages and then cities, but we still have a built-in need to identify with nature and to return to it from time to time. When we lose contact with our natural environment, we lose a part of ourselves, of our past, of our at-oneness with all living things. The danger is that in forgetting and neglecting the things of nature—or in taking them for granted—we run the risk of letting them be wasted and destroyed, of losing them forever.

Perhaps one of the best things we can do to help safeguard the natural environment is to get more people interested and involved in it. I think it is very important to pass legislation and to effectively enforce laws that will preserve and protect our wilderness areas. Of course we need the laws, but what we also need is to raise a generation of people who sincerely value, respect, and care about nature. I am particularly concerned with our youth, because the future of the earth will be in their hands. Fortunately, today's young people are already more interested in the environment than my generation was when I was growing up.

If, by our example, we teach our young people a deep respect for nature, I feel that we will make much progress toward the preservation of our earth. We will help to assure that our descendants will always be able to enjoy the brilliant colors of the leaves of autumn; the fresh morning air and the dew-coated grass of spring; the tracks of rabbits and deer in newly fallen snow; and the sight of wild geese as they fly in V-shaped formation to their breeding grounds in the Far North. We will enable future generations to experience the serenity of a quiet woods, to watch the unfolding of wild flowers, and to see the ripples on the water as a fish breaks the surface of a still lake. All these things, and many more, can be ours forever. All we need do is enjoy them—and protect them.

Earl W. Hunt has had a life-long fascination with the wilderness and its inhabitants. A self-taught naturalist, he first began to study wildlife as a boy growing up on a small farm in north-central Minnesota. By tracking animals through the woodlands and observing their habits, he acquired a detailed knowledge of the ways of wilderness life. Even after he moved to St. Paul in 1963 to pursue a career as a technician in a chemical research laboratory, Mr. Hunt did not lose touch with the natural world. Now he spends as much of his free time as possible at a cabin in the Minnesota woodlands, where he continues his observations of nature.

George Overlie is a talented artist who has provided illustrations for numerous books. Born in the small town of Rose Creek, Minnesota, Mr. Overlie graduated from the New York School of Design and began his career as a layout artist. He soon turned to book illustration and proved his skill and versatility in this demanding field. To create the subtle ink-and-wash drawings for *The Living Wilderness,* Mr. Overlie drew on his own experience as a sensitive observer of natural life.

The illustrations in this book were done on scratchboard, using a combination of wash and dry-brush. The typeface used in the text is 11-point Century, with headings in Grouch. The book was printed on 70# Mohawk Cream Vellum and bound in Baltic Vellum.